PRISONS, PRISONERS
AND THE LAW

PRISONS, PRISONERS AND THE LAW

BY

Dr J. J. McManus

Commissioner,
Scottish Prisons Complaints Commission

W. GREEN/Sweet & Maxwell
EDINBURGH
1994

First published 1995

ISBN 0 414 01019 1

A catalogue record for this book is
available from the British Library

Computerset by Mendip Communications Ltd.,
Frome, Somerset
Printed in Great Britain by Butler & Tanner Ltd.,
Frome and London

FOREWORD

by
Sheriff Principal Gordon Nicholson QC

For those of us who began our professional careers at a time when the writing of up-to-date textbooks on matters pertaining to Scots law was virtually unknown it has been a source of pleasure in recent years to see how more and more authors are turning their talents to the writing of books on more and more subjects which previously were not even written about at all. The present work by Dr McManus is of that kind.

Since the time of Hume, and indeed from even earlier, there have been several distinguished textbooks on the subjects of criminal law and criminal procedure but until now nobody has written in detail about the prisons and other institutions which mark the end of the criminal justice process for many offenders, nor about the law, both domestic and international, which governs the use which is made of such institutions and the way in which they are managed and run. Given the growing involvement in such matters of the courts, including in particular the European Court of Human Rights, it is especially timely to have a new book which explores the subject in depth but which does so with great clarity.

Dr McManus is particularly well fitted to have written this book. For many years he has taken a considerable interest in the subject of prisons and imprisonment. He has attended many international seminars and conferences on what the North Americans describe as "corrections". In 1988 and 1989 he made a distinguished and, at times, provocative contribution to the work of the Kincraig Review of Parole and Related Issues in Scotland, and he has now seen many of the recommendations of that Review incorporated in the Prisoners and Criminal Proceedings (Scotland) Act 1993. And, from 1988 to 1994 he was a member of the Parole Board for Scotland. He thus has brought to this book not only a background of academic study but also a sound practical knowledge of how prisons and imprisonment work in practice.

In my opinion this is a book which will be of interest and of relevance to many people. Plainly, it should be indispensable reading for all those who are involved professionally in the criminal justice system. But I suspect that it may also prove to be of interest to a much wider audience of people who simply wish to know a little more about one of the less visible, and often misunderstood, parts of that system. I can heartily recommend it to all potential readers.

Gordon Nicholson
Edinburgh, 1995

PREFACE

This is the first book on prisons law in Scotland. Had it been written five years earlier, the task of the author would have been much simpler. At that time there had been few substantial changes in the law for a considerable period, with the Act and the Rules both dating from 1952. Since 1989 however we have had the Prisons (Scotland) Act of that year, the Prisoners and Criminal Proceedings (Scotland) Act of 1993, the Criminal Justice and Public Order Act of 1994 and the Prisons and Young Offenders Institutions (Scotland) Rules 1994. Accordingly, the text has had to undergo several rewrites in order that the law may be presented as far as possible as at 1 November 1994. The flurry of legislative activity has of course made the text much more relevant and necessary. Various developments outlined in the text have rendered the law a much more significant element in the day to day life of prisoners than it has ever previously been. The form of the new law, reflecting as it does the commitments made in the Justice Charter and in the Scottish Prison Service's own publications to greater openness and accountability, makes the possibility of legal challenge much more realistic for prisoners. The substance of the new law reflects the great developments which have taken place both internally and internationally in the whole notion of prisoners' rights in the last two decades. The text is designed to meet the needs of all those involved with prisons, whether as staff, members of visiting committees, prisoners, prisoners relatives, friends or legal representatives. The text is primarily descriptive, though the author offers occasional comments on areas which may be ready for further development.

While the author of course accepts full responsibility for any errors or omissions which remain and for all expressions of opinion, he gratefully acknowledges the assistance of several people in bringing this project to fruition. Colin Reeves, Jinny Hutchison, Jim Patton and Maureen Killow of the Scottish Prison Service Secretariat provided assistance and information throughout the project; the University of Dundee gave the author sabbatical leave for a term in 1993–94 to enable the text to be written; and Sheriff Principal Gordon Nicholson read the text, offered comments and provided the foreword. To all of these and to the production staff at Greens, the author proffers his sincere thanks.

J. J. McMANUS
University of Dundee
1994

CONTENTS

Contents

TABLE OF CASES

ABBREVIATIONS

References to the most commonly cited Acts and Rules in the text are abbreviated as follows:

The 1952 Act	The Prisons (Scotland) Act 1952
The 1989 Act	The Prisons (Scotland) Act 1989
The 1993 Act	The Prisoners and Criminal Proceedings (Scotland) Act 1993
The 1994 Act	The Criminal Justice and Public Order Act 1994

CHAPTER 1

IMPRISONMENT IN SCOTLAND TODAY

The Early History of Imprisonment

Acts of the Parliament of Scotland make clear that there were   **01–01**
such things as prisons as early as the eleventh century. Until
the nineteenth century, however, the main use of prisons
was for the detention of debtors and the holding of persons
awaiting trial, execution or transportation. Imprisonment as
a punishment in itself was not a regular sanction, and did not
become one until transportation to the Colonies was brought
to an end when the Colonies were able to reject our rejects.

Scotland's response to the ending of transportation was   **01–02**
not a planned one. People who had been sentenced to be
transported, but on whom the sentence could not be carried
out, were held initially in the very ships which would have
carried them away. As it became clear that the ships would
never sail again, something had to be done. That something
was an expedient, but one which has grown into the prison
system which we have today. With some notable exceptions,
the same principle of expediency has characterised
developments in penal law and practice for much of
Scotland's subsequent history. Indeed, only in the period
since 1987 is it easy to detect evidence of coherent planning,
but even this had to start against the background of its
inheritance.

The early development of the prisons had been a   **01–03**
responsibility of the burghs, often to the chagrin of the
burghers who had had to meet the cost. The counties had had
no obligation to maintain prisons or to contribute to the
upkeep of the burgh prisons which might be used by them. A
statute of 1819 authorised the counties to make voluntary
contributions for the maintenance of the burgh prisons, and
there is evidence that at least some counties took pity on their
burghal neighbours. But the result was that the availability of
prisons was patchy throughout the country, and the
standards adopted in each of the areas were unique to the
area. When the English penal reformers Elizabeth Fry and
John Howard extended their mission to Scotland in the early
part of the nineteenth century, they were not only appalled

1

by what they saw, but also well enough connected and respected to have official note taken of their report. This signalled the beginning of the end for the local based system, and the start of a move towards the nationalisation and rationalisation of prison provision in Scotland. It was not only the influence of the campaigning English which helped to bring this about; there was also a strong involvement from native Scots reformers, some of whom, like George Brebner, the governor of Glasgow Bridewell, become influential throughout the penal world. Brebner's story is well told by one of his successors in the Scottish Prison Service, who himself contributed greatly to developments in Scotland before taking his mission south of the border (Coyle, "The Founding Father of the Scottish Prison Service", *Journal of the Association of Scottish Prison Governors* (1982), Volume 1 pages 7–14). In a later book, Coyle provides a more general overview of the early history of imprisonment in Scotland (Coyle, *Inside: Rethinking Scotland's Prisons* (1991)). When added to Cameron's work (Cameron, *Prisons and Punishment in Scotland* (1983)), we have available a reasonable record of the practices of early times.

The Prisons (Scotland) Act 1839

01–04   The reform movement started by paying attention to the legal and administrative structures of the prisons. The Prisons (Scotland) Act 1839 aimed to improve discipline within the prisons and gave to the High Court of Justiciary the duty of general superintendence over the prisons. A General Board of prisons was established to direct Scotland's one general prison, at Perth, and to supervise local prisons, each of which had a County Board appointed to take responsibility for day-to-day supervision and the appointment of staff. This arrangement lasted for 21 years, until the Act of 1860 abolished the General Board at Perth and replaced it with four managers, the Sheriff of Perth, the Inspector of Prisons for Scotland, the Crown Agent and a nominee of the Crown. County Boards were now to report directly to one of Her Majesty's principal Secretaries of State, who would also be advised by the managers of the prison at Perth.

The Prisons (Scotland) Act 1877

This process culminated in the Prisons (Scotland) Act of 01–05
1877, which transferred to the Secretary of State all
responsibility for prisons (section 5) and made prisons a
charge on central government funds (section 4). Section 6
made provision for the appointment of prison
commissioners, who were to report annually to Parliament
on their activities (sections 11, 12). Local involvement was to
be continued through the appointment of visiting
committees and the according of a power to sheriffs to visit
their local prisons, but section 17 specifically removed the
obligation on local bodies to maintain prisons.

Centralisation allowed for more or less coherent strategies 01–06
to be formulated and developed for the running of penal
establishments and gradually, therefore, for the slow
emergence of what could be called, at least *ex post facto*, a
penal philosophy. But the legal structure which was in place
by 1877 was, in effect, to outlast all the various philosophies
which came and went. Of course the Act was amended,
generally in bits and pieces and occasionally in larger
bits—like, for example, the Criminal Justice (Scotland) Act of
1949. The response to the frequent amendments has been to
consolidate the statutes from time to time, as in the Prisons
(Scotland) Act 1952 and, more recently, in the Prisons
(Scotland) Act 1989—which itself has already been amended
on three occasions (by the Law Reform (Miscellaneous
Provisions) (Scotland) Act 1990, the Criminal Justice Act 1991
and the Prisoners and Criminal Proceedings (Scotland) Act
1993). The result is that the basic statute regulating
imprisonment today can still be traced to the 1877 Act.
Legislative development has taken place in fits and starts
without the opportunity ever having been taken of a
fundamental rethink of the legal basis. This is not a great
testimony to the foresight of the drafters of the 1877 Act.
Rather, it is evidence of the fact that the law has not generally
been seen as relevant to the many developments which have
taken place in penal practices and establishments over much
of this time.

The structure of the law itself helped to make this possible. 01–07
In particular, the wide powers and discretions accorded to
the Secretary of State, and the lack of any notion of
"prisoners' rights" within the thinking of the time, ensured a
flexibility in the legal structure which, in the absence of

effective legal challenge, enabled developments to take place
without the form of the law being reassessed. The domestic
legal system made effective legal challenge difficult; it
seemed that the Secretary of State had power to do whatever
he wanted, and the prisoner no locus to bring any legal action
against him. Extra-legal challenges would be almost bound
to be either criminal offences or offences against prison
discipline. And, quite apart from being expressly denied the
right to vote by section 3 of the Representation of the People
Act 1983, convicted prisoners were not likely to be able to
excite public support in any claim for improvement of their
position. The fact is, however, that the climate has changed
considerably over the last 20 years. A combination of the
intervention of international bodies, like the European
Commission and the European Court of Human Rights and
the United Nations, the easier availability of access to
domestic courts by prisoners, developments in academic
thinking, the increasing professionalism and activism of
prison staff and, perhaps, the resort by prisoners to extra-
legal methods of voicing dissatisfaction with their lot has
ensured that changes had to take place in prisons. This time,
the changes have involved the law in an intimate way,
sometimes as a prompt, other times as a way of consolidating
changes occasioned by the other facts. It is necessary,
therefore, to look briefly at these factors.

Contemporary Context of Imprisonment

1. Academic Thinking

01–08   After generations of relatively abstract academic thinking in
the field of punishment—with notable exceptions like
Bentham's practical involvement in the design of the
Panopticon (the prison design which enabled an officer to see
all the prisoners in their cells while each prisoner could only
see the officer)—the emergence of the social sciences into
academia ensured that the question of punishment be
addressed as a practical as well as a philosophical one. By the
1960s it was the received orthodoxy that the perceived
advances in the social sciences enabled society to identify the
causes of crime and prescribe appropriate "treatments" to
solve the problem. The medical analogy was widely
accepted and had led to at least the rhetoric of "treatment"

being adopted in many countries, including Scotland (Prison (Scotland) Rules 1952, rule 5). Though perceived in most quarters as a more liberal approach to dealing with criminals, the "Treatment Model" in fact led to greater intervention with the freedom of the convicted person. Whereas in the retributivist model of punishment the length of time to be served in prison was determined purely by the nature of the offence and the offender's degree of culpability, the treatment model demanded a flexibility in sentencing, and in the administration of sentences, so that the criminal could be detained until the treatment was deemed to have worked.

Academic disenchantment with the treatment model grew   **01–09** alongside the "New Criminology" of the late 1960s. In particular, the idea that criminal deviancy could be equated with physical illness and responded to with the same approach ceased to make any sense when it was accepted that criminals were simply people who had been caught, processed and convicted for doing something which Society had decided, at least for the time being, should be defined as criminal. Given that societal definitions could be very fickle, though not perhaps as fickle as the processes which resulted in only a small proportion of those who actually committed the acts defined as criminal being traced, prosecuted and convicted, basing intervention on the notion of treatment was seen as at best misguided and at worst a cynical manipulation of the humane idea of treatment to cover the reality—Society's need to *control* those it did not like. Perhaps the rapidly approaching 1984 concentrated the minds of those who had read the Orwellian fantasy on the fact that many of the necessary pre-conditions for the all-controlling State were inherently present in this approach to punishment.

2. Legal Systems' Responses

(a) United States

Changes in academic orthodoxy are not renowned for   **01–10** having an immediate impact on the world of penal affairs, any more than on any other world. It had taken considerable time for the social sciences to impact at all on the practices of criminal justice systems. The radical nature of much of the new criminology made it even less likely that the anti-treatment approach would have any impact on how the courts or the prison administrators operated. But an early, if unlikely, ally was found in the shape of the American Supreme Court. In the celebrated case of *Re Gault*, 387 U.S. 1 (1967), the continued detention of a minor who had been alleged to have made an indecent telephone call was ruled unconstitutional since none of the due process requirements had been fulfilled before his detention on the grounds of his "delinquency". Until this case, the rehabilitative ethos of the juvenile court procedure had been seen as justifying departure from the due process requirements. In a book following this case, counsel for the child argued forcefully that the whole idea of detention for compulsory treatment was unconstitutional since, if effective, the treatment would remove the ability to deviate and thus deprive human beings of a basic right, the right to be different (Kittrie, *The Right to be Different* (1971)). The fact that no treatment had been found which could "cure" the majority of criminal deviancy only compounded the problem. People were being deprived of their freedom for a purpose which could not be achieved and which is of doubtful moral validity in any case. It may have been the failure of the system to produce a successful treatment which led to the court's decision, but counsel was arguing a much more crucial point. If the law's intervention in people's lives was to be limited only by the prospects of successful treatment, the very freedoms which the law exists to protect would be at risk.

01–11   The U.S. had, of course, adopted the treatment model in a more extreme way than Scotland and, indeed, most other countries. Thus, in the U.S., the majority of prison sentences were expressed in an indeterminate way. Convicted persons were sentenced to terms like "five to ten years" and their liberation date was determined by a variety of executive devices in accordance with perceptions of how the prisoners had responded to the treatment. They have now moved far from that approach, again showing total commitment to the prevailing orthodoxy, but that is a separate tale.

(b) Scotland and the United Kingdom

01–12   Scotland had espoused "treatment and training" as the official objectives of imprisonment and had introduced a parole scheme in 1968 (Criminal Justice Act 1967), but no attempt had been made, officially at least, to adopt treatment as the main aim of sentencing more mature offenders. The peak of our commitment to the treatment model can be seen in the childrens hearings system, introduced under the Social Work (Scotland) Act 1968, where at least there is an upper age limit of 18, after which the system can no longer restrict the person's freedom. In relation to other offenders we had, therefore, avoided the worst excesses of the U.S. system. Indeed, our brief experimentation with extended periods of detention for persistent offenders, corrective training and preventative detention, both introduced by the Criminal Justice (Scotland) Act 1949 and finally abolished by the Criminal Justice (Scotland) Act 1980, proved not only short-lived but also very unpopular because they offended against the judiciary's traditional sense of proportionality in sentencing. At the same time, however, the rhetoric of treatment had come to dominate official discourse about imprisonment and it fitted easily with the traditional paternalism which characterised the relationship between the prison system and the prisoner and which was embodied in the legal structure which accorded the prisoner only privileges rather than rights.

This distinction between rights and privileges has been a **01–13** crucial one in the development of prisons law in the U.K. Throughout their history, neither the primary nor the secondary prisons legislation made any reference to the notion that prisoners may have rights. Rather, the rules (mainly) accorded prisoners certain privileges, surrounded always with grants of associated discretions to the Secretary of State or the governor in relation to when these privileges could be exercised and when they might be withdrawn altogether. The basic assumption was that on admission to prison, the subject lost all rights. Anything then granted to him was a privilege, to which there was no entitlement and refusal of which thus gave rise to no legitimate complaint. It is nowhere clear that this was the result of a conscious decision by a draftsman or prison administrator schooled in the analytical jurisprudence of Hohfeld. Rather, it may, like the prisons themselves, just have grown up and owed more to the old notions of "outlawry", with its consequential deprivation of all legal status, than to any policy decisions. None the less, when legal challenges were mounted by prisoners, the administrators did attempt to rely on the distinction between rights and privileges, a distinction which the European Court of Human Rights felt not to be very useful in *Campbell and Fell* v. *U.K.* As will be seen below,

01–14 the 1994 Rules maintain the distinction, but identify clearly what are privileges and what are rights. Quite apart from the lack of legally enforceable rights accorded to the prisoner, Scotland, in common with its U.K. neighbours, lacked the mechanism of a supreme court which could be used to challenge the legislative structure of imprisonment. Accordingly, the Scottish courts had been given no opportunity to say anything about the conditions of imprisonment or to comment on the aims and objectives of the institution. English prisoners, on the other hand, had not been so easily deterred and managed to raise some issues in their courts. The results were not encouraging, even when the challenge was mounted on an alleged breach of the rules. Thus, in an *obiter* judgment, Goddard L.J. expressed what was to become the accepted ruling in relation to the enforceability by prisoners of the prison rules:

"[I]t seems to me impossible to say that if [the prisoner] can prove some departure from the prison rules which caused him some inconvenience or detriment he can maintain an action. It would be fatal to all discipline in prisons if governors and warders had to perform their duty always with the fear of an action before their eyes if they in any way deviated from the rules. The safeguards against abuse are appeals to the governor ... and ... to the Secretary of State, and those, in my opinion are the only remedies" (*Arbon v. Anderson* [1943] 1 All E.R. 154).

Lord Denning took this approach even further in his judgment in the case of *Becker v. Home Office* [1972] 2 Q.B. 407:

If the courts were to entertain actions by disgruntled prisoners the governor's life would be made intolerable. The discipline of the prison would be undermined. The Prison Rules are regulatory directions only. Even if they are not observed, they do not give rise to a cause of action.

01–15 There is nothing to suggest that Scottish courts, had they been given the opportunity, would have responded any differently. The structure of the prison law was essentially the same in the two jurisdictions, as was the policy decision not to accord private rights under public legislation save when the statute made clear that this was the intention of Parliament (*Pullar v. Window Clean Ltd.*, 1956 S.C. 13. What was needed was a materially different view of the relevance of the law to prison administration than that which had developed under the Scottish—or English—approach to the question.

(c) European Convention on Human Rights (ECHR)

This different view was taken by the European Commission and Court of Human Rights and the Council of Ministers. The U.K. had been one of the first to sign the Council of Europe Convention for the Protection of Human Rights and Fundamental Freedoms and to accept the jurisdiction of the court in cases raised under it. Once the right of individual petition was recognised by the U.K. in 1965, the way was open for prisoners to seek remedies where none had been available before. Many of the cases brought under the Convention have been raised by persons in custody. The most significant cases are reviewed below—and it should be noted that the majority of cases from the U.K. emanated from English rather than Scottish prisons. But, although practices between the two countries differed in some important matters as well as in details, our legal structures have been very similar and our acceptance of the ECHR as one United Kingdom binds all parts of the Kingdom to accept and implement the judgments of the court in all jurisdictions within the U.K. Accordingly, changes have been prompted in both systems by decisions of the Commission and the court.

01–16

More importantly, however, the availability of this external forum has had a wider impact than simply the individual decisions it has come to on prison matters. Not only have the domestic courts been affected by the knowledge that they may not have the last word on an issue (as, for example, in the case of *Tarrant*, discussed fully below), but also the prison policy makers themselves have, at least latterly, taken anticipatory steps to ensure that their practices accord with the requirements of the ECHR. As the jurisprudence of the Commission and the court has developed, and as the Council of Europe has developed more pro-active agencies under new treaties like the Convention establishing the Committee for the Prevention of Torture and Cruel and Inhuman Treatment or Punishment, it has become clear that the international community is committed to continuing improvements in penal conditions, not least as an indication of countries' commitment to improving human rights generally. Accordingly, the ECHR

01–17

has been a powerful force in changing the general climate in relation to prisoners' rights and seems likely to continue to prompt changes in this area. Initially perceived perhaps as a threat to our domestic arrangements, the ECHR is now viewed more as a challenge by professional prison administrators, committed to ensuring that practices in Scotland accord with all the international obligations which we, as a civilised country, have undertaken.

3. Prison Staff and Administrators' Contributions

01–18   The increasing professionalisation of prison staff has been a separate factor in the developments of the last two decades. Where previously the image of the prison officer was that of a "turnkey", whose only task was to ensure that the prisoners in his charge were kept securely and hard at demeaning work, the prison service of the 1990s has succeeded in improving the status of its staff and is increasingly ensuring that recruitment and training policies produce staff worthy of the status of professionals. Interestingly it was a committee appointed to look into the terms and conditions of appointment of prison staff in the late 1970s which led to the official abandonment of the "treatment model" in the U.K. The May Committee, which had among its membership the now Sheriff Principal Gordon Nicholson, found itself obliged to go much further than its remit may have suggested. Its recommendations included abandoning the notion of treatment and substituting "Positive Custody" as the main aim of imprisonment.

01–19   There was little immediate response to the report of the May Committee, but it helped to sow the seeds for developments which were to take place in the 1980s. These started with the prison service itself being restructured into a unified service, abolishing the almost complete divide between officers and governor grade staff, and putting all staff onto a salaried basis. But although this reorganisation was undoubtedly important, it would not necessarily have achieved much on its own. Indeed, without the next and final factor, it may be that nothing would have changed fundamentally in Scottish prisons.

01–20   As the notion of "positive custody" has been developed in Scotland, the role of the prison officer has become crucially important. In addition to performing the basic task, that of keeping in secure custody persons sent to prison by the courts, the staff have an obligation to create a climate which is conducive to the prisoner exercising choices which will improve the chance of not resorting to crime on release. Clearly, this implies a different relationship between staff and prisoners than that which is possible when all power lies on the side of the staff and prisoners are expected simply to do what they are told. Equally clearly, such a change in approach cannot be introduced overnight. It takes time not only for attitudes and expectations to change, but also for staff to be trained in the new role. Given the lack of attention traditionally paid to staff training when the job was perceived as simply that of the turnkey, the time involved may be significant. At least, however, the commitment has been made, and the change is well underway.

4. Prisoners' Contributions

The final factor in the process of change was the prisoners   **01–21**
themselves. It may be difficult for officialdom to admit it, but it seems very likely that an important catalyst for change in Scotland has been the series of prison disturbances which took place in the late 1980s. A variety of reasons for the disturbances, which affected most long-term adult prisons and included hostage taking and the destruction of property, has been put forward. Official sources suggested that the disturbances were orchestrated by small groups of hard core criminals intent on causing problems (see, for example, Report of Her Majesty's Chief Inspector of Prisons for Scotland into Prisoner Grievances at Peterhead Prison (March 1987)); prisoner-oriented accounts blamed prison conditions—poor visiting facilities, degrading facilities and oppressive regimes (*The Roof Comes Off*, Gateway Exchange, Edinburgh, undated). Whatever the cause, it was clear that something had to be done to give prisons a sense of direction, at least to prevent a recurrence of the horrific scenes that were regularly witnessed throughout Scotland. Prisoners—or at least some of them—were, it seemed, no longer content to stay quiet and obedient in the face of what some of them saw as a prison system which denied them any real say over their lives.

5. Outcome

The initial response of prison administrators and the   **01–22**
politicians was, perhaps understandably in view of the lack

of coherent planning which had gone into prisons, to see the incidents of the mid-1980s as individual problems caused by particularly difficult prisoners. For a period they pointed to "evidence" that this was the case. Thus poor conditions in prisons could be ruled out as a cause of the troubles since the new prison at Shotts, with excellent physical facilities, had suffered at least as much from the disruption as older prisons. Equally, they pointed to the liberalisation of regimes—as evidenced in the increased provision of visits and other facilities for prisoners throughout the system—as an indicator that it was not oppressive regimes which were causing the problem. The only possible factor, therefore, was individual prisoners intent on disrupting the system because they could not handle their sentences.

01–23   Perhaps it was the quality of some of the senior management of the Scottish Prison Service (SPS) which ensured that the analysis quickly became deeper than this. Incidents persisted, even when the identified troublemakers were relocated to very restricted regimes and isolated from other prisoners. The SPS finally decided that a fundamental rethink was required.

01–24   Starting with *Custody and Care* (Scottish Office, March 1988), the SPS has set out, in a series of well publicised documents, its new vision of what prisons should be about. The very fact that all of the documents are published and that everyone has been invited to contribute to the discussion of them betokens a new spirit of openness in a world previously characterised by almost obsessive secrecy. But not only do these documents adopt modern management terminology, they also outline a radically different approach to the basic task of prisons, given, of course, that their first task is to keep in custody those committed to them by the courts.

01–25   *Opportunity and Responsibility* (SPS, May 1990) best sums up this approach: prisoners are to be treated as responsible adults, who have choices about what they do with their time within the confines of the prison. The task of the prison service is to make available to prisoners a safe and secure environment in which they are encouraged to make use of such facilities as can be provided. These facilities are geared to assisting the prisoner to address any problems which may have contributed to the offending behaviour which has resulted in imprisonment. In all cases, attempts should be made to minimise the disruption to family life inherent in imprisonment and to impose on each prisoner the minimum amount of security and other restrictions required for safe and orderly confinement.

Whereas the old perception of the prisoner under the treatment model was of an irresponsible or "sick" person who needed to be helped by the staff within a regime which denied choices to prisoners and imposed internal discipline and restrictions on contact with the outside, more calculated to isolate people from the real world than prepare them for reintegration into it, the new stresses that prisoners are still fully human beings, albeit with their freedom temporarily restricted on account of their own actions or alleged actions. It is not suggested that the law has been the sole or even the main prompt for this approach to prisoners, but the new philosophy can be seen as perfectly compatible with the summary of the prisoner's legal position expressed in the famous judgment of Lord Wilberforce in *Raymond* v. *Honey* [1983] 1 A.C. 1: **01–26**

> **A convicted prisoner, in spite of his imprisonment, retains all rights not taken away expressly or by necessary implication.**

The changed status of the law is, however, reflected in the SPS documents. Both *Custody and Care* and *Opportunity and Responsibility* make reference to the need to update the legal structure of imprisonment, not only to reflect the new ideas, but also to remedy defects in the form and the content of the law which had become apparent over the years. **01–27**

Perhaps the clearest example of these defects was the Prison (Scotland) Rules 1952. Made under the authority of the Criminal Justice (Scotland) Act 1949, the Rules were amended on at least 25 occasions, but never consolidated. They continued to provide for sentences and practices long since abandoned—for example, preventative detention was still covered and visiting committees were specified as the only body which could authorise a prisoner to change his religion. As long ago as 1983 Her Majesty's Chief Inspector of Prisons for Scotland suggested that urgent steps should be taken to update and consolidate the Rules. It was perhaps a measure of perceptions of the importance of the Rules to the daily operation of the prisons that this was not finally done until 1994. **01–28**

The dawning of the new era has brought the law onto centre stage. It is perhaps as well that the policy change came first. New prison rules in the mid-1980s would not have gone **01–29** nearly as far as the 1994 Rules in incorporating the new sense of direction of the SPS. The service has now committed itself legally to delivering what it has so far promised in its own publications. In doing so it may have created a rod for its own back, but it is a clear measure of the level of commitment which exists to delivering the new regimes.

6. The Numbers Game

01–30   There can be little doubt that there has been a sea change in the approach taken by the SPS to the performance of its role in society. Unfortunately, however, it is not master of all its own proceedings. In particular, it has no control over two of the determinants of what it can do—the numbers of people committed to its care and the length of time for which it must keep them. Ever since the High Court of Justiciary lost its supervisory role in relation to prisons in the nineteenth century, there has been no direct point of contact between those who sentence people to prison and those who have to carry the sentence out.

01–31   Sheriffs still have the right to visit prisons to which they can commit people (Prisons (Scotland) Act 1989, section 15), but it seems that relatively few exercise this right regularly. Scottish prisons cannot refuse to take people validly committed to them. Dutch prisons are forbidden by law to admit more prisoners than they are certified to hold, and operate a "waiting list" system for short-term prisoners when the jails are full; the Republic of Ireland resorts to executive release by the Minister of Justice to avoid overcrowding. Scottish prisons are required to have elastic walls.

01–32   Various attempts, as described in Chapter 2, have been made to restrict the use of imprisonment as a sentence in Scotland, but there seems to have been no concerted attempt to control, on the basis of a consistent policy, the total numbers committed, the reasons for their committal or the length of time for which people are committed. The independence of the judiciary has been prized over all other considerations. The result has been that our prison population has fluctuated widely, in a way which has been generally unpredictable and often inexplicable even *ex post facto*. Overall, the trend has been for the population to increase, though there have been periods of reduction. There have also been periods when the numbers in particular categories of prisoner have increased or decreased in relatively consistent, though again not predictable, directions. Thus, in general, there has been a significant reduction in the number of remand prisoners in the period since 1985, and a reduction in the average sentence of young offenders in the same period. On the other hand, the average length of adult sentence has increased by 25 per cent between 1982 and 1992. The numbers of fine and compensation order defaulters sent to prison rose to a record number in 1988, but have fallen significantly since then. Given that both the law and operational requirements demand that these categories of prisoner are accorded different treatment, the prison system has had to make constant changes to the use made of individual prisons and parts of prisons in order to accommodate these developments. The current use of each establishment is outlined in Appendix 1.

Trends in the prison population are best demonstrated in   **01–33**
tabular form (Tables 1–4).

One factor which has, however, been consistent   **01–34**
throughout is the apparent Scottish tendency to make use of imprisonment to a far greater extent than almost all of our European neighbours. Scotland has no greater (or lesser) crime rate than anywhere else in Europe. Yet, according to Council of Europe figures, we consistently commit more people per head of our population to prison every year than all other member countries except Turkey (Table 5).

This, of course, is the most damning way to present the   **01–35**
statistics from Scotland's point of view. These figures are the *detention* rates. Every time a person is sent to prison, on remand or on conviction, it is counted, and the total number is then divided by the population of the country. Thus, if someone is received into prison on remand and subsequently sentenced to a period of imprisonment, this counts as two detentions. When we add the information that the average period spent in custody in Scotland is the lowest in the Council of Europe, we can begin to take some comfort from the figures. The fact is, of course, that because of our rule limiting custodial remands to a maximum of 110 days before a trial commences, we may be counting the same person many times while our neighbours would still have that person in custody awaiting trial on the first charge!

Nonetheless, there are no grounds for complacency. We   **01–36**
still have to ask why it is that imprisonment is used so often in Scotland. Indeed, it seems particularly difficult to justify

TABLE 1
Direct Receptions into Adult Prisons by Sentence Length

Year	Total	<90 days	91 days to 6 months	6–18 months	18–36 months	36+ months	Life	Aver (exc life)
1982	7992	4861	717	1678	373	337	26	206
1985	8864	5300	899	1746	379	525	15	242
1986	8598	5104	859	1746	421	443	25	227
1987	7975	4674	958	1581	367	378	17	219
1988	7984	4377	1121	1683	378	392	33	233
1989	7619	4397	875	1577	341	399	30	233
1990	7551	4199	945	1599	353	430	25	236
1991	7951	4430	1008	1683	374	437	19	244
1992	8543	4327	1369	1937	366	519	25	258

TABLE 2
Direct Receptions to Young Offender Establishments by Sentence Length
(Excluding Detention Centre Sentences)

Year	Total	<3 months	3–6 months	6–18 months	18–36 months	36+ months	Life	Aver days
1985	2359	1012	288	815	116	118	10	242
1986	2593	1144	347	869	121	104	8	225
1987	2064	913	274	665	128	75	9	222
1988	2160	1082	336	592	95	53	2	189
1989	2651	1537	346	608	94	59	7	167
1990	2719	1500	353	658	120	82	6	194
1991	2356	1167	335	655	105	88	6	209
1992	3041	1492	488	798	142	109	12	217

TABLE 3
Remand Receptions to Scottish Prisons

Year	1985	1986	1987	1988	1989	1990	1991	1992
No.	16782	18766	17111	15000	14281	15168	13127	13548
Av.time	n.a.	n.a.	20.0 days	20.6 days	19.7 days	18.1 days	21.4 days	23.7 days

TABLE 4
Fine and Compensation Order Defaulters Received into Prison

Year	1985	1986	1987	1988	1989	1990	1991	1992
Nos.	9877	10538	10846	11150	9622	8592	6915	8010

[Sources: Scottish Prison Service Annual Reports and Scottish Office Statistical Bulletins. It should be noted that the counting periods changed from financial years to calendar years in 1989, but this has little effect on the trends.]

Table 5

Detention Rate per 100,000 population and Average length
of Imprisonment in Council of Europe Countries as at
February 1, 1990

Country	Detention Rate	Time (months)
Northern Ireland	112.3	n.a.
Scotland	94.8	2.8
England	93.3	n.a.
Luxembourg	92.6	6.8
Wales	92.5	n.a.
Portugal	85.0	10.0
FRG	83.8	6.6
Austria	83.0	4.1
France	81.2	6.8
Finland	71.7	4.2
Belgium	71.0	4.5
Denmark	61.0	n.a.
Sweden	60.0	n.a.
Ireland	56.0	n.a.
Italy	55.1	n.a.
Greece	48.7	n.a.
Netherlands	44.2	3.8
Cyprus	40.2	4.1
Iceland	39.8	3.6

[Source: *Prison Information Bulletin* 16 (June 1992), Council of
Europe, Strasbourg. The average detention period for Scotland has been calculated using the figures given in the
annual reports for Scotland.]

the use of short periods of prison. Presumably people are
imprisoned at least partly because they are perceived as a
threat to the community. If this is the case, it is not likely that
the degree of threat will recede speedily. Accordingly, it is at
least arguable that short periods of imprisonment are more
difficult to justify than longer ones, and therefore that
Scotland's practice is even more out of line with the rest of
Europe than at first appeared.

Unless some method of controlling the numbers 01–37
committed to prisons is found, or a method of ensuring that
there are always resources to match whatever numbers are
committed, there will continue to be difficulties in delivering

a quality of service to prisoners which meets the aspirations of the SPS and, indeed, the domestic and international legal obligations imposed on the service. This topic is outside the scope of this book, just as it appears to be outside the influence of prison administrators. But it is such a crucial determinant of what prisons can do that it deserved this mention.

7. Likely Future Developments

01–38   It is unlikely that domestic or international legal bodies have reached the end of their concern with developing penal law. Indeed, the new Prison Rules in Scotland, coupled with increasing openness in regard to general matters of penal administration, make it likely that there will be more rather than less involvement by legal institutions in the running of prisons. Although, as the concluding chapter of this book argues, this is not necessarily the best way in which to develop a rational penal strategy, it is bound to be a continuing factor in the process, and one which can be harnessed, by a proper understanding of what law and legal processes have to offer, to help create a prison system which is both just and effective in achieving what society wants from it.

CHAPTER 2

HOW TO GET TO PRISON

It is not necessary to be convicted of an offence in order to be   **02–01**
sent to prison. Almost 20 per cent (929 out of a total of 5180 on
January 14, 1994) of the average daily population of Scottish
penal establishments have not been sentenced as a result of a
criminal conviction. To be fair, most of them have been
remanded in custody, awaiting trial or sentence on a criminal
charge. There are some, however, who are not alleged to
have been involved in anything criminal at all. Civil
prisoners, as they are known, can be committed for contempt
of court or failure to pay a fine imposed therefor, breach of an
interdict, failure to comply with an order under section 45 of
the Court of Session Act 1988, under section 4 or 6 of the Civil
Imprisonment (Scotland) Act 1882 or by warrant under
section 1(1) of the Law Reform (Miscellaneous Provisions)
(Scotland) Act 1940. In addition, people can be committed
under the Immigration Acts without committing a criminal
offence. The numbers involved in each of these categories are
always small, rarely exceeding an averge of one per day. A
brief summary of the special Rules governing their treatment
is given below (Chapter 4). It thus remains the case that
prisons are predominantly for holding those charged with,
or convicted of, criminal offences.

Attempts have been made over the years to restrict the   **02–02**
numbers of persons sent to prison both pre- and post-trial.
Successive governments, aware not only of the financial cost
of imprisonment but also of its adverse effects on people
imprisoned, have attempted through legislation to ensure
that it is used as a sentence or as a pre-trial or pre-sentence
measure only in cases where no other option is appropriate.
In the case of post-conviction disposals, imprisonment is
statistically a minority disposal, albeit one which is growing
in popularity. Thus, in 1992, custody was the main disposal
in only 7.4 per cent of all cases, with a fine, constituting the
main disposal in 74 per cent of all cases, still by far the most
popular choice. Unfortunately, however, disposals other
than imprisonment have come to be talked of as "alternatives
to prison", thereby giving the impression that imprisonment
is the normal response and anything else is somehow

"letting the criminal off". The dangers of this approach contributing to inflation in sentencing are manifest.

02–03 Much concern is being expressed currently about the matter of pre-trial remands in custody or on bail. The police in particular are often to be heard complaining vigorously about accused persons being granted bail on one charge and going on to commit further offences while awaiting their trial. The blame usually falls on the Bail (Scotland) Act 1980, though little consideration is given to the failure to implement the provisions of another 1980 Act, the Criminal Justice Act, which authorised the provision of bail hostels as a halfway house between remand in prison and remaining fully in the community.

02–04 It falls to be considered, therefore, what the law is regarding those who constitute the overwhelming majority of our prison population under the two main headings of remand prisoners and sentenced prisoners.

Remand Prisoners

02–05 The Bail (Scotland) Act 1980 and the guidelines issued under the Act by the then Lord Justice Clerk, Lord Wheatley, in the case of *Smith* v. *McC.*, 1982 S.C.C.R. 115 (*sub nom. Smith* v. *M.*, 1982 S.L.T. 421) make clear the logical position in a system holding to the presumption of innocence, that "An accused should be granted a bail order unless it can be shown that there are good grounds for not granting it". Equally, persons found guilty or convicted of offences but not sentenced immediately should only be remanded in custody pending sentence or disposal if that is the only option.

02–06 Lord Wheatley did not believe that a complete catalogue of grounds for refusal of bail could be compiled. He did, however, indicate that previous convictions on their own were not sufficient grounds for refusing bail, but the protection of the public and the administration of justice might demand refusal in any particular case. The best list of valid grounds for refusing bail which can be compiled from his guidelines, but which must be applied in the individual circumstances of each case, might read as follows:

> The nature of the alleged offence, if especially serious;
> The previous criminal history of the alleged offender;
> Whether or not the alleged offender was in a position of

special trust at the time of the alleged offence (i.e. was already on bail or ordained to appear in relation to another matter, was subject to a probation or community service order, on parole or licence, or was subject to a deferred sentence);
Any alleged intimidation of witnesses;
Absence of a fixed abode;
Reasonable grounds for suspecting that the accused will not turn up for trial.

1. Practice

Notwithstanding the seeming restrictiveness of these guidelines, the remand population in Scottish prisons grew to an alarming extent in 1986, with the result that SACRO set up a working party on the subject in that year. Since the report of the working party was published (*Bail and Custodial Remand* (SACRO, 1987)), though not necessarily because of the report and the publicity it attracted, the remand population has fallen but remains at levels which give cause for concern. In particular, it should be noted that, in most years, there are almost as many people received into prison on remand as there are on conviction. With an average period of only some 23 days spent on remand, the disruption to individuals' lives and the cost in administration must be disproportionate to the good results obtained in a considerable proportion of these cases.

02–07

TABLE 2.1
Remand Receptions into Scottish Prisons

Year	Total
1985	16782
1986	18766
1987	17858
1988	16583
1989	15262
1990	14447
1991	14602
1992	13158

But it is not simply the numbers of such prisoners that create problems for Scottish prisons. Remand prisoners themselves pose particular challenges to penal establishments.

02–08   First, the law governing their detention is different from that governing sentenced prisoners, again reflecting the presumption of innocence, and they are supposed to be kept apart from such prisoners (rule 14 of the Prisons and Young Offenders Institutions (Scotland) Rules 1994). The details of the law are discussed below (Chapter 4), but the fact is that accommodation to keep remand prisoners separate from other classes of prisoner is not readily available in many places and the maintenance of markedly different regimes is accordingly problematic.

02–09   Secondly, the psychological needs of remand prisoners are also markedly different. The sentenced prisoner generally accepts his sentence and settles down to it reasonably quickly. The unconvicted ones live in hope that they will not be convicted and unsentenced ones that they will not be sentenced to imprisonment. They all tend to be very short term prisoners, and to be kept among a population which is, by its nature, constantly changing. Since their common feature is the fact that they are unsentenced, it is generally difficult to allocate them in accordance with their (alleged) offence. Accordingly, there can be a mixture of the genuinely innocent with those guilty of serious or minor offences, first offenders and multiple offenders, young and old, stable and not so stable. In all they pose particular managerial problems, and few prison staff would mourn if the numbers of remand prisoners were greatly reduced.

02–10   The SACRO report suggested various steps that could be taken to reduce the number of persons committed to custody before trial and sentence and also recommended the establishment of a separate remand service as a part of the SPS. Little seems to have been done, either in law or in practice, to improve the situation of remand prisoners in the period since the report was published, though it is understood that moves are now afoot in a variety of places to establish bail hostels as an alternative to incarceration. The treatment of this group in custody is an area which now requires urgent attention.

2. Backdating of Sentences

02–11   Time spent in custody before conviction, or between conviction and sentence, is not automatically deducted from any prison sentence imposed. Until the passage of the 1993 Act, courts, when imposing a custodial sentence, were required to "have regard to" any time spent in custody before sentence (Criminal Procedure (Scotland) Act 1975, section 218 (solemn procedure), section 432 (summary procedure)). These sections, as amended by section 41 of the 1993 Act, now require the court to specify the start date of the sentence and, if the person has spent time in custody before sentence, to state the reason if it decides not to order that the start date should be earlier than the date of sentence. This provision represents a compromise between the Thomson Committee recommendation (*Criminal Procedure in Scotland*, Second Report Cmnd. 6218 (1975)), that sentences should always be backdated to the date when an intimation to plead guilty was made, and the Kincraig Committee majority recommendation (*Parole and Related Issues in Scotland*, Cm. 598 (1989), paragraph 10.22), that all sentences should be backdated to the initial remand in custody unless there were special reasons to order otherwise. The new provision may be read as implying that all sentences should be backdated, but there is room for continuing the old law as it had emerged, somewhat confusingly, in practice. Thus, in *Doolan* v. *Lockhart*, 1987 G.W.D. 12–434, it was held that it was possible for a court to have regard to a period spent in custody without taking it into account. Equally, courts had identified factors, like co-operation with the police on arrest (*Aird* v. *H.M. Advocate*, 1987, unreported), early intimation of a guilty plea (*Grant* v. *H.M. Advocate*, 1988 G.W.D. 34–1439) and remand for reports following a guilty plea (*Morrison* v. *Scott*, 1987 S.C.C.R. 376), as situations where a sentence should be backdated. It remains to be seen how the practice of the courts will develop in the light of the new statutory provision.

Sentenced Persons

1. Young Offenders

(a) Persons under the age of 21

As the law has attempted to ensure that people are sentenced to imprisonment only as a last resort, it has introduced categorisation of convicted persons in accordance with a variety of criteria seen as relevant to this aim. In the first   **02–12** place, there has been a series of statutes regulating sentencing of young offenders. Starting with the Prevention of Crimes Act 1908 and culminating in the Criminal Justice (Scotland) Act 1963, the law gradually provided for a total prohibition on the sentencing of persons under the age of 21 to imprisonment. Instead, they were to be sentenced to a variety of different types of detention, though, since the Criminal Justice Act 1988, all are now sentenced simply to detention. Borstal, a creation of the 1908 Act, was abolished in 1980; the detention centre (the "short sharp shock" so beloved of armchair penologists) departed in 1988. Properly speaking, therefore, the terms "prisoner" and "imprisonment" should only be used in relation to persons over the age of 21. However, for the sake of convenience, the terms will be used indiscriminately herein, except where different provisions apply to those under the age of 21.

02–13   Secondly, the law has striven to ensure that even these amended forms of detention are not used capriciously for young offenders. The current position is, under the Criminal Procedure (Scotland) Act 1975, as amended, that no young offender can be sentenced to detention unless the sentencing judge is of the opinion that no other sentence is appropriate (sections 207(3), 415(3)). Before reaching such a conclusion, the judge must consider the background of the offender (sections 207(3)(4), 415(3)(4)), and will almost inevitably have commissioned social inquiry reports on the offender. Reasons for a decision that custody is the only appropriate sentence must be recorded when the sentence is imposed by a court other than the High Court.

02–14   When a judge is dealing with an offender in this age group who has failed to pay a fine, the alternative period in custody cannot be imposed unless the offender has been given the opportunity to pay the fine under the supervision of a social worker and has been represented in court by an agent.

(b) Children

02–15   In dealing with persons under the age of 16 (or 18, where the person is subject to a supervision order from a childrens hearing), there are further restrictions on imposing custodial sentences. The vast majority of such children are, of course, dealt with by the childrens hearing system, and panels have no power to order the detention of a child. (They can, of course, order that a child be subject to residential supervision under section 44(1)(*b*) of the Social Work (Scotland) Act 1968, but this is not a "custodial disposal".) However, the 1968 Act leaves the Lord Advocate with the power to prosecute children in the normal criminal courts, a power which is generally exercised only where the child is accused of a particularly serious offence. On a finding of guilt in such a case (the terms "conviction" and "sentence" are replaced by "finding of guilt" and "order" by section 429 of the 1975 Act), the court in solemn proceedings can, under sections 205 and 206 of the 1975 Act, order the child to be detained for a specified period, or without limit of time, in a place to be determined by the Secretary of State. Such a place may, but need not necessarily, be a penal institution. More commonly they are detained, at least initially, in the secure wing of an approved school. In summary proceedings, the court may order the child to be detained in residential care by the appropriate local authority (1975 Act, section 413). The release of such children is, as will be seen below (Chapter 6), subject to different rules from that of other sentenced persons.

(c) Unruly Children

Only in exceptional circumstances may a person under the **02–16** age of 16 be confined in a prison. Sections 24 and 297 of the 1975 Act allow a court, when remanding or committing for trial a person aged between 14 and 16, to remand or commit that child to a prison only when the court is satisfied that the child is so unruly or depraved that he cannot be dealt with by a place of safety order, or committed to a remand centre. Provisions exists for the Secretary of State to specify conditions which must be met before a court can reach this conclusion, but this power has not been exercised (Children Act 1975, sections 70(a), 108(2)). Nevertheless, there has been a welcome and consistent reduction in the use of such certificates since Her Majesty's Chief Inspector of Prisons focused attention on the issue and, in particular, on the inappropriateness of prisons being used for this purpose in 1984. The average daily population of such children in prison has now fallen to less than one. Though each local prison may be required to hold them, it is normal for Longriggend Remand Institution to take almost all of them.

(d) Numbers of Young Offenders

As is evident from the tables in Chapter 1, the numbers of **02–17** young offenders in custody has varied markedly over the last decade. The abolition of Borstal sentences seems to have been a major factor in this, though precise reasons for the fall are not known. Despite its political popularity, detention centre was abolished in 1988, and all young offenders now receive the same sentence of detention.

2. Offenders Over the Age of 21

(a) Direct Sentences of Imprisonment

02–18   Less vigorous attempts have been made to exclude this age group from custodial sentences, but there are restrictions on the use of imprisonment for them. Anyone not previously sentenced directly to custody (i.e. excluding those who have been sent to prison in default of payment of a fine and those remanded to prison pre-trial or pre-sentence), can only be so sentenced after the court has received a background report, usually in the form of a social inquiry report (1980 Act, section 42). The sentencing court in summary cases must certify the reason why it does not consider that a non-custodial disposal is appropriate (section 42(2)). Otherwise, attempts to avoid the use of imprisonment have centred on creating alternative sentences, like the community service order (CSO), and ensuring that probation orders are strictly enforced. There was, however, nothing expressly in the legislation introducing the CSO which required courts to impose Community Service only as a direct alternative to custody. Such a provision was inserted into the Community Service by Offenders Act 1978 by section 61(3) of the Law Reform (Miscellaneous Provisions) (Scotland) Act 1990, but in the absence of detailed guidelines about when custodial sentences are appropriate, it may be that we are not much further forward. The position might be clarified if the sentencing commission mooted in the discussion paper *Sentencing and Appeals* (Scottish Office, 1994) were to be created.

(b) Fine and Compensation Order Defaulters

02–19   Imprisonment remains the ultimate sanction for failure to pay a fine or compensation order. On imposing a fine, the court must, unless the offender has sufficient means to pay immediately, has no fixed abode or there is "other good reason", give the offender time to pay (1975 Act, section 396(1)). Unrepresented first offenders cannot, however, be immediately imprisoned for failure to pay a fine without having been given the opportunity of applying for legal aid (Criminal Justice (Scotland) Act 1980, section 41(1)). If time to pay is given, the court cannot order the alternative period of imprisonment to be served on default unless there are special circumstances, and such circumstances must be recorded (1975 Act, section 396(4)). Courts may also order that the offender subject himself to supervision from a social worker, under a fine supervision order, until the fine is paid (1975 Act, section 400(1)).

On default, or on the application of the fined person if his **02–20** circumstances have changed, a court is convened to inquire into the offender's means (a means inquiry court) (1975 Act, section 398(1)). Such a court can remit the fine, vary any instalments or impose a period in custody on the following scale:

Fine (in pounds)	Max. Period in custody
<£50	7 days
50–100	14
100–400	30
400–1000	60
1000–2000	90
2000–5000	6 months
5000–10000	9
10000–20000	12
20000–50000	18
50000+	24

(1975 Act, section 407)

The alternative period in custody cannot be imposed on a **02–21** young offender unless there has been a fine supervision order in place or the court is satisfied that such an order would be impracticable (1975 Act, section 400). Experiments are currently underway with "supervised attendance orders", where selected offenders may be given the opportunity to undertake a work programme as an alternative to imprisonment or detention. Otherwise, courts can only impose the alternative period in custody. They have no power to substitute the alternative sentences which the original sentencing court could have imposed. Attempts to give courts this power failed, in the Law Reform (Miscellaneous Provisions) (Scotland) Bill 1990, and have not so far been resurrected.

02–22   Fine defaulters account for a substantial proportion of admissions under sentence into Scottish prisons. In 1993 they constituted 9,148 of the total of 21,628 persons received under sentence into Scottish prisons. The average period they spend in prison is comparatively short, but they cause disproportionate problems for prison administrators. Thus, for example, they are entitled to be released at any time on payment, by themselves or by someone on their behalf, of the sum outstanding. That sum reduces proportionately for each day they spend in custody. Since they are also entitled to one-half conditional release, if sentenced after October 1, 1993, or one third remission, if sentenced before that date, the computation of sentence to be served or amount to be paid can be complicated (see Chapter 6 below). Implementation of the government's proposals, in its 1989 consultation paper *Fines and Fine Enforcement*, would greatly ease the problems this group creates.

(c) Courts Martial

02–23   The Secretary of State has power to decide where a person sentenced by court martial should serve the sentence, and has decided that the whole or part of any military sentence of imprisonment in the U.K. should be served in a civil prison (Imprisonment and Detention (Army) Rules 1979 (S.I. 1979 No. 1456) rule 14). Once received into a civil establishment, persons sentenced by courts martial are treated in exactly the same way as those sentenced by civilian courts. Sentences of detention are normally served in military establishments, which have separate rules and regulations governing them.

(d) Minimum Period of Imprisonment

02–24   Summary courts are not allowed to impose sentences of imprisonment or detention of less than five days (1975 Act, section 425). They may, however, make use of legalised police cells, where available, for up to five days on conviction (section 425(2)), and may also order that a person be detained within the confines of the court for the balance of the day of the court appearance (section 424). A day's detention must end in time to allow the person to travel home by public transport or, at the latest, 8.00 p.m.

Conclusion

People can thus come into custody for a variety of reasons. In **02–25** Scotland the relatively small number committed for reasons other than (alleged) breaches of the criminal law is small, reflecting enlightened decisions made as early as the 1930s to restrict severely the use of imprisonment as a means of enforcing compliance with the civil law (see, for example, the Hire Purchase and Small Debt (Scotland) Act 1932). Nonetheless, as will be seen below, separate provision has to be made within prisons for the treatment of such prisoners.

In relation to those committed under the criminal law, **02–26** however, Scottish practices do not seem to reflect any coherent policy. In particular it may be thought that the high numbers imprisoned for failure to pay fines is anomalous. Scottish Office research reveals that the main reason for non-payment of fines is poverty. Individual fine levels are supposed to be set by reference to the means of the offender (1975 Act, section 395(1)): though no official hierarchy of penalties exists, it seems not unreasonable to posit that imprisonment is not the logical next highest punishment after the fine. Accordingly, there is clearly something wrong with a system which imposes fines that people cannot pay, and then uses imprisonment as the only available sanction for non-payment. Similar criticisms may be advanced over the lack of alternative provisions for those awaiting trial or sentence, for whom the total freedom of bail is not adjudged appropriate. For prison, the ultimate sanction of the law, to be the only available option in such cases, is not sensible. Finally, it might be thought that repeated short sentences of imprisonment imposed for comparatively minor offences are a manifestly ineffective way of tackling the problems of alcohol and other drugs which are common factors in the commission of minor offences.

Whatever the reasons, it seems likely that Scottish **02–27** practices in relation to the decision to deprive people of their liberty will only undergo fundamental change if either Parliament or the High Court is prepared to depart from its previous stance and issue more direct instructions or guidelines to sentencers about the use of custodial disposals. The *Sentencing and Appeals* discussion paper proposes a sentencing commission for sheriff courts, and the High Court is to have access to a data base of sentences passed for categories of offence. Both of these initiatives may prompt further developments, but it should not be assumed that the inevitable outcome will be a reduction in the use of custody. Experience elsewhere, notably in the U.S., has been that sentencing guidelines lead to an increase in the prison population. Given that the U.S. has an imprisoning rate in excess of 500 per 100,000, more than four times Scotland's rate, perhaps this is not a useful model. What might more realistically be looked for is closer co-operation between the various arms of the criminal justice system. It could not but help if sentencers were more aware of the reality of the sentences they impose, and were encouraged to take a greater interest in following up the outcome of individual sentences. Experience is the main teacher of our sentencers, but experience can only be a teacher if the pupil is allowed to find out what the outcome of previous actions has been and forced to face the consequences of the mistakes made.

CHAPTER 3

THE LEGAL STRUCTURE OF IMPRISONMENT: BASIC SOURCES AND PERSONNEL

Sources of the Law

1. Primary Legislation

The main primary legislation governing imprisonment is **03–01**
contained in the Prisons (Scotland) Act 1989, and the
Prisoners and Criminal Proceedings Act 1993. The latter Act
deals mainly with the matter of release from custody, and is
treated in detail in Chapter 6.

The 1989 Act was a consolidating measure, as was its **03–02**
predecessor, the Prisons (Scotland) Act 1952. Consolidation
was required on both occasions because of the tendency to
change the law relating to prisons in a piecemeal fashion, a
tendency which shows few signs of abating. Accordingly, it
has often been difficult to find a concise statement of the
legislation governing prisons, and it is to be hoped that
further consolidation exercises are not left as long as the
delay between the last two. Better still would be a wholly
new Act, reflecting the changes in policy in relation to
imprisonment, demonstrating and reinforcing its coherence,
and ensuring that easy access is available to everyone who
wishes it.

2. Secondary Legislation

(a) Statutory Instrument

The 1989 Act continues the practice of its predecessors in **03–03**
empowering the Secretary of State to make regulations
under the Act for the discharge of the duties accorded to him
by it. It is now clear that, for the most part, these powers must
be exercised by means of statutory instrument, subject to the
negative resolution procedure in general, save when
attempting to alter the parole qualifying periods or
delegating authority to the parole board in classes of case
(1989 Act, section 42, 1993 Act, section 45). The main body of
these regulations has recently been substantially updated

and promulgated as the Prisons and Young Offenders Institutions (Scotland) Rules 1994 (S.I. 1994 No. 1931).

03–04   The approach adopted, as well as the individual rules in this new set of Rules, are markedly different from their predecessors. They accord prisoners many more rights, are far more comprehensive in their coverage and may thus lend themselves much more readily to forming the basis for legal action to ensure their enforcement. It is not, however, likely that they would give rise to any right of action for damages for breach of statutory duty. In two English cases, arising from very similar legislative provision, the House of Lords held that, in the absence of an express provision giving prisoners the right to seek private law damages for breach of statutory duty, no such right could be inferred (*R.* v. *Deputy Governor of Parkhurst Prison ex p. Hague,* and *Weldon* v. *Home Office* (conjoined appeals) [1992] 1 A.C. 58). This decision is consistent with Scottish authorities in other areas of public law duties (*Pullar* v. *Window Clean Ltd*, 1956 S.C. 13). The new Scottish Rules do not grant any such express right, though they could found a stronger argument for an implied one than their predecessors, particularly when taken in conjunction with the statements in the policy documents which preceded them. Nonetheless, judicial review continues to offer the most likely mechanism for successful challenge to penal practices under the Rules.

03–05   Perhaps more importantly, at least in terms of demonstrating real commitment by the Scottish Office to the promises made in *Custody and Care* and *Opportunity and Responsibility*, the new Rules contain many provisions which were previously regulated by secret standing orders. Not only do they improve on the substance of the previous dispensation (for example, in doubling the minimum availability of showers for prisoners (rule 22(2))); they also make the provisions open for prisoners and their representatives to see. Thus there is a requirement, in rule 5, that the Rules and any directions made under them shall be made readily available to officers and prisoners. In all, therefore, they represent a significant advance on the pre-existing system. They are considered in greater detail below.

(b) Directions

03–06   Under the previous dispensation, much reliance was placed on a third tier of regulations, known as standing orders. These orders were not generally available to prisoners or their representatives and were used to give detailed instructions about the management of prisons and prisoners. In this they effectively regulated much of the daily life of prisoners and covered crucially important matters like security categories. Their secrecy was thus hard to defend, and had begun to disintegrate under assault from the ECHR. Thus the orders relating to prisoners' correspondence were published in response to a series of ECHR cases relating to censorship of correspondence, and in particular a complaint that prisoners did not know what they could and could not write, and to whom. Although the initial response of the Prisons Department to these adverse rulings was grudging, their final response is encouraging.

Recognising the need for some flexibility and a need for **03–07** very detailed regulation in some areas, the 1993 Act amended the 1989 Act to allow the Secretary of State to supplement the prison Rules by the issue of directions (1989 Act, section 39(8)–(11), as added by the 1993 Act, section 25). Directions can only be issued for purposes provided in the Rules, though they may create discretions for prison governors or officers (section 39(8)), and they may provide for derogations, within limited situations, from other rules (section 39(9)). The Secretary of State is obliged to publish all directions in such manner as he considers appropriate (section 39(11)), and to make them available to staff and prisoners (rule 5). As will be seen below, provision has been made for relatively extensive use of this power, but it is a circumscribed one and the provision for publicity will at least provide for both availability of and accountability for the directions so made.

(c) Standing Orders and other Instructions

There will still, no doubt, be matters which will need to be **03–08** regulated in these ways, but they should be fewer in number and much less important in content than before because of the increased amount of detail in the Rules themselves, and the provision of the power to make directions under the Rules. In the face of the explicitly authorised rules and directions, it will be more difficult for prison administrators to argue that other forms of regulation have any *vires*, and impossible to claim that they can authorise any departure from an express requirement of a rule or direction. Accordingly, the situation which arose in the English case of *Raymond* v. *Honey* [1983] 1 A.C. 1 should not recur. There, a prison deputy governor, relying on standing orders, stopped a letter which a prisoner had written in relation to court proceedings. The English High Court held that "standing orders, if they have any legislative force at all, cannot confer any greater powers than the regulations which ... must themselves be construed in accordance with the statutory power to make them". The Scottish courts had reserved opinion on the *vires* of standing orders in *Leech* v. *Secretary of State for Scotland*, 1991 S.L.T. 910. With the appearance of the new Rules and directions, this matter should not now need to be resolved.

3. International Treaty Obligations

(a) The Council of Europe

(i) The ECHR: the Commission, Court and Council of Ministers

03–09   The Council of Europe has taken a variety of initiatives which have had considerable impact on the conditions of detention in member states which have accepted the various conventions. The most significant Convention has been the European Convention on Human Rights and Fundamental Freedoms (1950), which came into force in 1953 as the Council's way of advancing the United Nations Universal Declaration of Human Rights (1948). Signatories undertake to guarantee to protect the rights outlined in the Convention to all persons within their jurisdiction, and give authority to the European Commission, Court and Council of Ministers to interpret and apply the Convention in individual cases.

03–10   The Convention has not been incorporated into Scots law. Nonetheless, it has had a significant impact on the development of prison-related law and practice in Scotland. The U.K. has accepted the right of individual petition under the Convention. Accordingly, any individual alleging violation of any article of the Convention can bring an action against the U.K., subject to the Rules of procedure of the Convention. Given the Convention's origins as a method of ensuring that the atrocities perpetrated during the Second World War should never be repeated, the substantive provisions of the Convention have particular relevance to the conditions of detention and many of the cases brought under the Convention have concerned detainees. Articles 3 (relating to cruel and inhuman treatment and punishment), 8 (covering restrictions on correspondence), 6 (right to natural justice in proceedings restricting freedom or rights) and 12 (covering right to marry and family life) have been the main grounds of action by detainees. In the absence of any other statement of fundamental rights within the U.K. legal traditions, and of any legal mechanism for asserting such rights, the Convention has offered particular hope to persons in the U.K. In response to adverse rulings under the Convention, the U.K. government has altered both Rules and practices in relation to penal establishments. Accordingly, the Convention has exercised a significant, though legally indirect, influence on the development of penal law.

(ii) The European Prison Rules

Following on a United Nations resolution in 1957, the **03–11** Council of Europe adopted "The European Standard Minimum Rules for the Treatment of Prisoners" in 1973, and updated these Rules as "The European Prison Rules" in 1987. The Rules have no legal force in member states. Rather, they are intended as a stimulus to member states in developing their own rules and practices. Their impact on the new Scottish Rules is easy to detect.

(iii) The Convention for the Prevention of Torture and Inhuman or Degrading Treatment or Punishment

Under this Convention, the Council of Europe established in **03–12** 1987 a separate mechanism for ensuring that contracting parties comply with Article 3 of the ECHR (prohibition of torture, inhuman or degrading treatment or punishment). The Committee for the Prevention of Torture, etc., (the CPT) is entitled under the Convention to carry out inspections of all detention facilities in signatory states. Under Article 11 of the Convention, the CPT reports the results of its inspections, in confidence, to the government of the member state involved. Publication of the report and any response by the government is at the discretion of the government, save in exceptional circumstances, when the CPT may make a public statement about what it has seen. The only example of this so far is the *Public Statement on Turkey* (CPT, December 15, 1992). Most member states have so far agreed to publication. It is clear from these published reports, and from the published annual reports of the CPT, that the committee adopts a wide interpretation of its remit. It is not bound by the court's (very narrow) interpretation of Article 3, but neither is the court bound by the CPT's interpretation. The CPT's role is thus a pro-active one, geared to assisting member states to improve the conditions of detention and to avoid any possible violation of Article 3. A very good example of its work is the published report on the CPT visit to the U.K., a critical report (based only on visits to English detention facilities), to which the U.K. government has responded in a positive and public way (The Report is published as *CPT/Inf(91) 15*, and the U.K.'s responses as *CPT/Inf(91) 16* and *(93) 9*). It is likely that this committee will become an increasingly important agent for improvements in conditions of detention.

(b) United Nations

03–13 The UN has not had the same direct impact on the development of U.K. prisons law as the Council of Europe, which has been the main mechanism through which European states have fulfilled the obligations undertaken as a result of UN initiatives. Thus, although the U.K. has ratified the International Covenant of Civil and Political Rights drawn up in 1966, it has not accepted the right of individual petition, presumably on the grounds that the ECHR already achieves the same effect. Equally, the UN has adopted the Body of Principles for the Protection of all Persons under any Form of Detention or Imprisonment, but this has not necessitated any direct change within the U.K.

Personnel of the Prison Systems

03–14 Until the passage of the Criminal Justice and Public Order Act 1994, the whole of the Scottish Prison Service was required to be under the direct control of the Secretary of State for Scotland. The 1994 Act, however, creates the possibility of the involvement of the private sector in providing escort services, running parts of prisons or running whole prisons, subject to restrictions imposed in the Act. Accordingly, it is necessary to outline the two different personnel systems which may be involved in the prison systems.

A. Directly Managed Prisons

1. The Secretary of State for Scotland

The 1989 Act vests all powers and jurisdiction in relation to   **03–15**
directly managed penal establishments in the Secretary of
State for Scotland (section 1). "Directly managed" is defined
negatively in the 1994 Act as meaning any prison which is
not contracted out (section 112(7)) and "contracted out"
means any establishment or part of an establishment or
function in relation to which the Secretary of State has
entered into a contract with another person for that other
person to run or perform (section 106(4)). In the directly
managed sector, the Secretary of State may, with the consent
of the Treasury, appoint such officers, inspectors and
servants as he thinks fit (section 2). He has a specific power to
appoint governors, matrons and other officers, including
medical officers (section 3(1)), a duty to appoint a Church of
Scotland chaplain (section 3(2)) and a power to appoint
ministers of other denominations (section 9—see below). He
has full legal estate in every penal institution (section 36),
powers to buy and sell land for them (sections 37, 38), and
powers to make contracts and do all other acts necessary for
the maintenance of the buildings and those detained in them.

Section 4 provides for regular inspection of all aspects of   **03–16**
directly managed penal establishments by, or on behalf of,
the Secretary of State. He must make regular reports to
Parliament on the condition of prison and prisoners,
including a statement of the work carried out in
establishments (section 5(1)(2)), and must present an annual
statement of all punishments inflicted within each
establishment, and the offences for which they were inflicted
(section 6). In practice, an annual report is submitted,
covering all aspects of prison conditions and, since 1990,
giving details of plans for the future development of each
establishment.

The Act gives specific powers to the Secretary of State in   **03–17**
relation to the confinement, treatment and discharge of
persons confined to custody. These powers must generally
be exercised through the Rules and directions, though the
right to make standing orders, or to issue directions or other
kind of instructions, is expressly retained in the new
subsection (8) of section 39 of the 1989 Act, inserted by
section 25 of the 1993 Act. Relevant rules and directions are

discussed in detail in the following chapter. Some powers—like the one in section 19 to set up remand institutions—have never been exercised.

03–18   It is thought that the granting of "agency status" to the Scottish Prison Service, from April 1993, should distance the Secretary of State from the day-to-day running of even the directly managed penal establishments. Nothing in this grant, however, can alter the legal position of the Secretary of State under the Act or the Rules. It is purely a managerial arrangement, which leaves the powers and responsibilities of the Secretary of State as outlined above.

2. Minister of State for Home Affairs

03–19   The Secretary of State for Scotland commonly is assisted in discharging his responsibility for penal affairs by a Parliamentary Under-Secretary of State who acts as Minister for Home Affairs.

3. The Scottish Prison Service

03–20   From April 5, 1993, the SPS has assumed agency status under the Government's policy for devolving management responsibility for public bodies. In conformity with the plans announced in *Organising for Excellence*, the organisational review of SPS published in 1990, the SPS is run by a Prisons Board which consists of the Chief Executive, the Deputy Chief Executive, four departmental heads within the SPS, and two lay, non-executive directors. All board members are appointed by the Secretary of State. The board is assisted by civil servants and several seconded staff from the SPS. The SPS headquarters are at Calton House, 5 Redheughs Rigg, South Gyle, Edinburgh.

4. Prison Governors

03–21   Each directly managed penal institution has appointed to it a governor, who may have other governor-grade deputies or assistants. The numbers and grades of governors in each institution are generally determined by reference to the number and type of prisoners held in the establishment. Governor-grade personnel also hold posts in the training establishment and at headquarters.

03–22   The SPS became a "unified service" in 1986, with the aim of recruiting all new members of staff at grade 8 and allowing movement through the next seven grades to the most senior position of governor 1. A staffing structure review in 1994 will lead to the introduction of a subdivision of uniformed officers into security staff and residential staff, and to changes in the grading structure generally. Meanwhile staff of grades 8 to 6 wear uniform and those of 5 to 1 constitute the governor grades. It has not proved possible to recruit all ranks from the lower ranks, with the result that occasional open competitions are still held for recruitment straight to grade 5. All training for governor grades is organised through the Scottish Prison Service Training Organisation, which is based near Falkirk.

The main statutory responsibilities of governors, which, **03–23** under section 33A of the 1989 Act as inserted by section 116 of the Criminal Justice and Public Order Act 1994, and rule 3(1), normally means any officer of a governor grade or, in the absence of a governor grade, the most senior officer present in the prison at the time and authorised by the governor or, in some circumstances, any officer of the prison, have increased greatly under the new Rules. Originally they were to visit the whole prison and every prisoner at least once each 24 hours, draw the attention of the medical officer to any prisoner requiring treatment, give the medical officer a daily list of prisoners complaining of illness, give the chaplain and medical officer a list of prisoners confined to their cells, and keep records of the admissions to and liberations from the prison (1952 Rules, rule 31). Now, in addition to these, there is a host of provisions ranging from those relating to assisting the maintenance of family ties for prisoners (rule 33), through establishing an appropriate system of privileges for prisoners (rule 40), to providing reasonable opportunities for prisoner recreation outside normal working hours (rule 76). These are considered in more detail in the next chapter. In addition, governors have a general responsibility for the running of establishments, including the supervision of other staff and of all aspects of the regime. In carrying out all their duties, governors have a specific obligation to seek to eliminate all forms of discrimination (rule 4).

5. Uniformed Staff

Uniformed staff of directly managed prisons are recruited by **03–24** examination and interview, undergo an initial training course, usually at the SPS college near Falkirk, and remain under training for the first year of their employment. They may be employed at any establishment and transferred from place to place during their service. Officers are obliged to conform to the Rules and to orders issued by the Secretary of State and to obey the lawful instructions of the governor (rule 127). They must not take part in any business or pecuniary transaction with or on behalf of a prisoner without the authority of the Secretary of State, or bring in or allow to be brought in to the prison any article for a prisoner without the permission of the governor (rule 128). Subject to directions given by the Secretary of State, a governor may, when he has reasonable grounds for suspecting that an officer has concealed anything which may be prejudicial to security, good order or discipline, order the carrying out of a search of an officer or any property of that officer within the prison. Any such search must be carried out by two officers of the same sex as the officer being searched, and should be done outwith the sight of any other person as expeditiously and decently as possible (rule 130). Officers may not receive any unauthorised fee or gratuity in connection with their employment or have any interest in any contract or any person tendering for a contract in relation to the prison (rule 129).

03–25   The provisions which permitted officers to be required to live in prison quarters do not appear in the new Rules. In any case, officers have in practice been allowed to live where they like, within reasonable travelling distance of their establishment, since 1986.

03–26   The Rules also restrict officers in communicating with the media and other persons about matters relating to the officers' employment, and officers are forbidden, without the authority of the governor, to make any public pronouncement relating to the administration of any institution to which the Prisons (Scotland) Act relates, or to any person lawfully confined therein (rule 131). All officers are subject to a code of discipline, issued under the authority of the Rules (rule 132). The current code is dated July 1993.

03–27   In all other regards, officers had the same employment rights as ordinary employees until the passing of the 1994 Act. Section 127(1) of this Act makes it unlawful for anyone to induce a prison officer to withhold his services as such an officer, or to commit a breach of discipline. Any such inducement would constitute an actionable breach of duty owed to the Secretary of State, who may seek compensation for loss or damage occasioned by the breach of duty (section 127(2) and (3)). As a corollary to this, section 128 provides for the Secretary of State to create, in consultation with any representatives of those working in the prison service, a mechanism for establishing rates of pay and conditions of employment in the service. Only medical officers in Scottish prisons are exempt from these provisions (section 127(4)(b)). Unlike prison officers in England and Wales, Scottish prison officers are not accorded the status of constables in the exercise of their duties.

6. Civilian Staff

Prisons may also employ civilian staff as instructors, **03–28** tradespeople, secretaries and drivers. Under section 41A of the 1989 Act as inserted by section 152(2) of the 1994 Act, civilian staff in directly managed prisons may be authorised to conduct non-intimate searches of any prisoner to ascertain whether the prisoner has any unauthorised property in his possession. Reasonable force may be used in the execution of this duty, and governors must take steps to notify prisoners as to who the authorised civilian staff are.

7. Chaplains and Prison Ministers

Section 3(2) of the 1989 Act requires the Secretary of State to **03–29** appoint to each prison a chaplain, who must be a minister or licentiate of the Church of Scotland. In addition, section 9 permits the Secretary of State to appoint ministers of other denominations to visit a prison where the number of adherents of those other denominations justifies this. Both the Act and the Rules use the terminology of "denomination" throughout, thus impliedly excluding religions other than Christianity. However, rule 35(1) makes clear that all religious and moral beliefs may be catered for in arrangements to be made by the governor.

Prisoners are entitled to attend such services or meetings **03–30** of their own denomination as may be held within the prison. They may also receive visits, outwith the sight and hearing of officers, from the chaplain or visiting minister, unless the chaplain or visiting minister requests otherwise or the governor considers that it would be prejudicial to the interests of security or to the safety of the minister for an officer not to be present (rule 38). Governors must provide such books, literature and other materials as they consider appropriate for prisoners' religious needs and prisoners are allowed, as far as practicable, to keep such things in their personal possession and to engage in the practices of their religious denomination (rule 39).

03–31   Chaplaincy services are organised under two full-time chaplains, usually one from the Church of Scotland and one from the Roman Catholic Church. There is in addition a chaplaincy board, consisting of representatives of various denominations, which provides general support and encouragement for religious activities within penal establishments.

8. Medical Officers

03–32   The Secretary of State is required to appoint to each prison medical officers, being medical practitioners duly registered under the Medical Acts (section 3(1)). He must make such arrangements for the provision of medical services as he considers necessary for the prevention of illness, the care of persons suffering from illness and the after-care of such prisoners (rule 24). Appointments may be on a full-time or part-time basis. There seems to be a growing practice of appointing full-time medical officers, though there is a considerable body of opinion which argues that part-time appointments are better for ensuring that the appointees remain in touch with professional developments and practices in the wider community. A review of medical services in prisons has recently been carried out by the SPS.

(a) General Powers

03–33   Each prisoner must be examined by the medical officer as soon as practicable, and no later than 24 hours after reception into prison (rule 8(2)). Thereafter, at such times and with such frequency as the medical officer judges necessary, he must attend prisoners who complain of illness (rule 25). Both the governor and any other officer are obliged to bring to the attention of the medical officer any prisoner whose condition appears to merit it (rule 26).

03–34   The medical officer is empowered to call in, or refer the prisoner to, any other medical practitioner or specialist, or to require the governor to make arrangements for the treatment of any prisoner at a medical facility outwith the prison (rule 27). In appropriate cases, the medical officer may also arrange for reports to be obtained on a prisoner who appears, to the medical officer, to be suffering from a mental disorder which would justify transfer of the prisoner to a mental hospital under terms of the Mental Health (Scotland) Act 1984, section 71. The governor is obliged to submit such reports, one of which may be by the medical officer, to the Secretary of State (rule 31).

When a prisoner is placed under mechanical restraint or is **03–35** subject to cellular confinement, the medical officer must visit that prisoner as soon as practicable and at least once every 24 hours thereafter while the confinement continues (rule 28). If the medical officer forms the opinion that any prisoner should be subject to confinement in special conditions, should not participate in specified activities, or should only so participate subject to certain conditions, or should not be subject to cellular confinement or the application of any form of restraint allowed under the Rules, he must notify the governor accordingly, and the governor shall give effect to the medical officer's opinion (rule 29(1)). Medical officers are obliged to report, in the first instance to the governor, on any matter affecting the prison or the treatment of prisoners which requires attention on medical grounds; if the matter remains unattended, a report should be made to the Secretary of State (rule 29(2)(3)). The medical officer is also obliged to notify the Secretary of State if, on medical grounds, a prisoner is totally and permanently unfit to be detained further in prison, his life is likely to be endangered by continued detention in prison, or his health is such that he is unlikely to survive his sentence (rule 29(3)(4)).

The medical officer must maintain a record of the health **03–36** and medical treatment given to each prisoner, and it must be transferred with the prisoner if he is moved to another prison (rule 32). In the event of a prisoner becoming seriously ill or injured, or being admitted to an outside hospital, the governor is required to ask the prisoner if he wishes a relative or friend informed of this; in the case of young offenders under 18, the governor does not require the consent of the prisoner (rule 30).

(b) Specific Powers

In addition to these general powers, the medical officer is **03–37** accorded a variety of specific powers by the Rules. Thus, under rule 7(5), he can grant an exemption from the requirement that a prisoner must have a bath or shower on admission; either the governor or the medical officer can require a prisoner to share a cell if they think it desirable (rule 15(2)(b)); the medical officer can exempt a prisoner, on medical grounds, from the duty to keep a cell clean and tidy (rule 16(3)(a)); he can refuse a prisoner the right to wear his own clothes because they are not suitable on medical grounds (rule 18(2)(b)); he can order special food in addition to or in place of the regular prison diet (rule 21(5)); only the medical officer can order a prisoner to have his hair cut or to shave or not to shave (rule 22(3)); the medical officer can exempt a prisoner from working (rule 68(2)(a)); he can order an end to cellular confinement of a prisoner (rule 29(1)(d)) and order the use of restraints on a prisoner to prevent self-injury (rule 83(5)), or the removal of restraints ordered by the governor (rule 29(1)(e)). The medical officer is under an obligation to inform the governor of any prisoner who is pregnant and likely to give birth during the period of her imprisonment (rule 115(1)). Before the release or transfer to any place of a prisoner receiving treatment or under the supervision of the medical officer, the medical officer must examine that person and certify whether he is fit to travel. No one may be allowed to travel if the medical officer does not certify him as fit, though untried prisoners and others who do not consent to remain in the prison if otherwise entitled to discharge cannot be kept against their will on medical grounds alone (rule 118).

03–38   Prisoners have no general entitlement to consult a doctor of their choice. Untried and civil prisoners may, however, be attended by a doctor or dentist of their choice, provided that they meet the full cost of any treatment (rule 31), and be visited by a registered medical practitioner for the purposes of any proceedings in respect of which they are committed to or detained in prison (rule 56). Prisoners who are appealing against sentence or conviction, those who are convicted and awaiting sentence, those who are serving a sentence but are also subject to a further charge, and those detained while the Crown is appealing against a sentence may also be visited by a doctor of their own choosing, but only in relation to matters involved in the pending legal proceedings (*ibid.*).

03–39   All prisons have the services of such dental, optical and chiropody facilities as is thought fit. Most also have psychiatric services available, usually on a sessional basis, and psychological facilities either on a full- or part-time basis.

9. Social Workers

Social work services are provided in each prison by the local **03–40**
authority within the area of the prison. There is no specific
obligation on governors to provide social workers, but rule
33 requires that governors ensure that prisoners are given
reasonable assistance to maintain and develop relationships
with family and friends, and with other persons and agencies
outwith the prison as may best offer assistance during the
period in prison and in preparation for and after release.
Equally, rule 73 allows governors to arrange for counselling
appropriate for the needs of prisoners.

10. Education Staff

Most establishments contract for the services of full-time or **03–41**
part-time educational staff, who are employed by the local
authority of the area of the establishment. In late 1994,
educational services were the subject of competitive
tendering.

11. Visiting Committees

The 1994 Rules provide a new constitution for visiting **03–42**
committees, with effect from January 1, 1995.

(a) Appointments

Sections 8 and 19(3) of the 1989 Act require rules to be made **03–43**
for the appointment of a visiting committee to each penal
establishment. Under section 19(3), appointments to
committees for institutions holding persons under the age of
21 are the responsibility of the Secretary of State, while rules
made for the implementation of section 8 in relation to adult
establishments give the appointing power to specified local
authorities, but under a restriction that a minimum of
one-third of the appointees must not be members of the
council which appoints them (rule 133(3)). Under the new
Rules appointments are open-ended, though members may
resign at any time and may also be removed from office by
the appointing authority or by the Secretary of State if, in the
view of either, the member has failed satisfactorily to
perform his duties, becomes incapable of performing the
duties, is convicted of a criminal offence or his conduct is
such that it is not fitting that he should remain a member, or

the member has a direct financial interest in the prison contrary to rule 140 (rule 133(6)). Chairmen of committees are under an obligation to report to the appointing council any case in which it is thought that termination might be appropriate (rule 133(7)). Members of visiting committees may be paid allowances in respect of loss of earnings and travelling expenses; officers of the committees may also be paid a remuneration (1989 Act, section 8(3)). No member of a visiting committee may have a direct financial interest in any contract for the supply of goods or services to the prison for which the member is appointed, or for any other prison (rule 140).

(b) Functions of Visiting Committees

03–44 The Act (section 8(2)) requires that the functions of the committees shall be detailed in rules, but specifies that these shall include a requirement for members to pay frequent visits to the prison, hear any complaints made by prisoners and report any matter to the Secretary of State which the committee considers expedient. In addition, the section empowers any member of the committee to visit the prison at any time and have free access to any part of the prison, and to every prisoner.

(i) Meetings

03–45 The Rules require the committee to appoint a chairman and deputy chairman from among its membership, each for a period of three years, and a clerk, who must not be an officer of the Secretary of State, at its first meeting (rule 134(1)). It is required to meet at the prison at least once every three months (rule 134(3)), may appoint sub-committees for carrying out any of its duties (rule 134(4)), and must fix a quorum of not less than one-third of its total membership for the purpose of any proceedings, including the proceedings of a sub-committee (rule 134(5)). The committee must keep minutes of its proceedings and send copies of such minutes to both the governor of the prison and the Secretary of State (rule 134(7)).

(ii) Visits

03–46 Rule 135(1) provides a general statement of the role of the committees:

> A visiting committee shall co-operate with the Secretary of State and the Governor in promoting the efficiency of the prison and shall inquire into and report to the

Secretary of State upon any matter in which he may ask it to inquire.

In fulfilling this function, at least two members of the committee are obliged to visit the prison at least fortnightly. The committee is charged with bringing the attention of the governor to any matter it deems expedient to refer to him, and, if the governor does not remedy any matter so reported within a reasonable time, reporting this to the Secretary of State (rule 135(2)). It is required to pay particular attention to the state of the premises and the food and drink provided to prisoners, record its findings on each visit, and send a copy thereof to both the governor and the Secretary of State (rule 135(3)). In addition, it must also discharge such other duties as the Secretary of State may assign to it (rule 135(4)). Members are entitled to inspect any of the records of the prison, except personnel records, prisoners' records and security manuals or other papers which have implications for security, and must record particulars of any such inspection in their minutes (rule 138). The committee must submit an annual report to the Secretary of State as soon as possible after the end of March in each year (rule 139).

(iii) Complaints
The second main function of the committees is to hear and **03–47** investigate any complaint which a prisoner may make to it (rule 136). Complaints can be heard outwith the sight and hearing of an officer, unless either the prisoner or the committee member requests otherwise (rule 136(2)). The committee's formal response to any complaint is limited to recording its findings in its minute book, providing a copy to the governor and the Secretary of State, and informing the prisoner orally of its findings (rule 136(3)). Prisoners are entitled to request to see the visiting committee at any time, and an officer to whom such a request is communicated must convey it without delay to the governor, who must then inform the next member visiting the prison of all outstanding requests to be seen (rule 102). Prisoners may also write to the committee, and any such letter must be posted without delay (rule 103).

12. Association of Scottish Visiting Committees

Scottish Visiting Committees have formed themselves into **03–48** an association for the purposes of advancing their own training and co-operation in making representations to the

SPS. The powers of the committees have been considerably reduced in recent times. Thus, under the previous dispensation (old rule 45), they had authority to adjudicate on allegations of serious disciplinary breaches by prisoners, and to award punishments. This power is not mentioned in the new Rules. It had in any case not been regularly exercised in Scotland after the decision in the English case of *R.* v. *Home Secretary, ex p. Tarrant* [1985] Q.B. 251. The withdrawal of this power created an opportunity for committees to develop their other roles unhindered by prisoners' perceptions of the committee as part of the disciplinary system. While some committees have succeeded in doing this, the overall reputation of the committees has not improved. The changes to the appointment system, and the stricter requirements in terms of frequency of visits and meetings introduced by the 1994 Rules, may provide a new impetus for the committees to become a force in Scottish prisons.

13. Sheriffs and Justices of the Peace

03–49 Sheriffs and justices of the peace are entitled to visit and inspect any prison within their jurisdiction, or in which any person confined for an offence committed within their jurisdiction may be confined (1989 Act, section 15(1)). Communications with prisoners on such visits must be confined to the subject of the person's treatment in prison (section 15(2)). Sheriffs and justices do visit prisons, albeit with varying regularity, but it has not been common for prisoners to request to see them or for the judges to involve themselves in this way in complaints about prison treatment.

14. Her Majesty's Chief Inspector of Prisons for Scotland (HMCIP)

03–50 As a result of the recommendations of the May Committee, an independent prisons inspectorate was established in 1981 and express statutory authority for the appointment was given in the Criminal Justice Act 1982 (section 6A), now consolidated in section 7 of the 1989 Act. Appointment is by Royal Warrant (section 7(1)). The main duty of the post holder is to inspect or arrange for the inspection of prisons in Scotland (including legalised police cells), and report to the Secretary of State, concentrating particularly on the treatment of prisoners and conditions in prisons (section 7(2), (3)). Section 7(2) has been amended by section 104(2) of the 1994 Act to give HMCIP a duty to inspect the conditions under which prisoners are transported or held in pursuance of prisoner escort arrangements, and to report to the Secretary of State on them. The Secretary of State may also refer specific prisons-related matters to the Chief Inspector and direct him to report on them (section 7(4)). The Chief Inspector is obliged to submit an annual report to the Secretary of State and this must be presented to Parliament (section 7(5)).

To stress the independence of the inspectorate, the Chief   **03–51** Inspector and his staff are located at Saughton House, away from the headquarters of the SPS. A triennial inspection programme has been adopted and it has become established practice for the Secretary of State to publish the report on each inspection carried out, along with his response to any recommendations made by the Chief Inspector. The Chief Inspector is assisted in his work by two seconded prison governors and other administrative staff. In addition to routine inspection activities, the inspectorate has reported on an investigation into disturbances at Peterhead prison and conducted a review of social work and chaplaincy services in penal establishments. These reports have also been published. The inspectorate has no function in relation to complaints or grievances of individual prisoners.

15. Parole Board for Scotland

Section 20 of the 1993 Act authorises the appointment of a   **03–52** parole board, whose function it is to advise the Secretary of State on any matter referred to it by him in connection with the early release or recall of prisoners. The constitution and functions of the board are fully covered in Chapter 6.

16. Local Review Committees

Constituted by rules made under section 18(5) of the 1989   **03–53** Act, local review committees only function in relation to parole eligible sentences imposed before the coming into effect of the 1993 Act in October 1993. The committees, consisting of the governor or his representative, at least one social work member, and at least one independent member, act as a filter in the parole process. Only cases recommended by the committees, or which, though not recommended, pass either the Prediction Score or Sift tests (discussed fully in Chapter 6), are referred to the parole board for consideration for release. A member of the committee other than the governor interviews prisoners whose cases are being considered, in order to assist each prisoner to present his case for parole. The committees will cease to function when the number of cases to be considered under the pre-1993 provisions is such that parole board members can carry out all the interviews.

B. Contracted Out Prisons and Functions

03–54   The 1994 Act empowers the Secretary of State to create a new category of officers (to be known as "prison custody officers", who may, *inter alia*, perform escort functions); to enter into contracts with other persons for the provision of such prison custody officers; to enter into contracts with other persons for the running of prisons or parts of prisons, the performance of custodial functions at directly managed prisons and the provision of new prisons. The Secretary of State retains ultimate responsibility for contracted out functions and prisons, but there is no requirement that he should assume legal estate in any contracted out facility, and the powers of officers employed by parties entering into contracts with the Secretary of State are more limited than those employed within directly managed prisons. Contracted out facilities will be governed by sections 107–112 of the 1994 Act as well as by the 1989 Act and the rules made thereunder. The main differences between the private sector provision and the public sector are as noted below.

1. The Secretary of State

03–55   The 1994 Act empowers the Secretary of State to enter into arrangements with any person for the provision of prison escort functions, for the running of a prison or part of a prison by that person, for the provision of particular functions at a directly managed prison, or for the provision of a new prison. In each case, the Secretary of State retains a function in the approval of staff appointed for the performance of any of these duties. In relation to escort arrangements, the Secretary of State must appoint a prison escort monitor, a Crown servant with responsibility for reviewing the arrangements and reporting on them to the Secretary of State, investigating any allegations against officers, and reporting on any breaches of discipline by prisoners under the control of such escorts (section 103(1)), and the Chief Inspector of Prisons is obliged to inspect and report upon the conditions in which such prisoners are held or transported (section 103(2)).

2. Director and Controller of Contracted out Prison

Instead of a governor, each contracted out prison must have a director who is a prisoner custody officer appointed by the contractor and specially approved by the Secretary of State (section 107(1)). In addition, there must be a controller, a Crown servant appointed by the Secretary of State (section 107(4)). A director's powers are generally the same as the powers of a prison governor under the 1989 Act, but he may not inquire into any disciplinary charge brought against a prisoner, conduct the hearing, or make, remit or mitigate any award in relation to such a charge or, save in an emergency, order the removal of a prisoner from association or authorise the use of special cells or the application of special control or restraint (section 107(2) and (3)). A controller has the duty of keeping under review, and reporting to the Secretary of State on, the running of the prison, and investigating any allegations against officers employed at the prison (section 107(4)(a)(b)). The contractor is under an obligation to give all reasonable assistance to the controller in the performance of his functions (section 107(5)). **03–56**

Where it appears to the Secretary of State that a director has lost, or is likely to lose, control of a contracted out prison, or part of it, and that it is necessary in the interests of preserving the safety of any person or preventing serious damage to any property, the Secretary of State may appoint a Crown servant to act as governor of that prison for a specified period. Such a governor has all the powers of a director and controller. Both the making and the termination of an appointment of a governor in these circumstances must be notified as soon as practicable to the contractor, the director and the controller (section 111). **03–57**

3. Prison Custody Officers

Any person wishing to act as a prison custody officer, whether in performing escort functions, or custodial duties, or both, must obtain a certificate that he has been approved for the performance of such duties by the Secretary of State (section 114). Schedule 6 to the 1994 Act empowers the **03–58**

Secretary of State to issue such certificates only when he is satisfied that the applicant is a fit and proper person to be so certificated, and has been trained to an appropriate standard. The certificate may be suspended by an escort monitor, controller or governor, as appropriate, and subsequently revoked by the Secretary of State if he considers that the person is no longer a fit and proper person to exercise the function(s). The intentional making of a false statement and the reckless making of a statement which is false in a material particular in order to obtain a certificate are criminal offences, with a maximum fine, on summary conviction, not exceeding level 4 (Schedule 6, paragraph 5).

03–59   Prison custody officers, acting in pursuance of prisoner escort arrangements, have the power to search prisoners for whom they are responsible, and any person in or seeking access to any place in which such prisoners are, or are to be, held. In relation to the latter, the officer may only require the removal of outer coats, jackets, headgear and gloves (section 104(1) and (2)). The officer must also search an offender if ordered to do so under section 395(2) of the 1975 Act (power of summary court to order the search of an offender when a fine has been imposed) (section 104(4)). The officer has a duty to prevent prisoners escaping from lawful custody, prevent or detect and report upon the commission by prisoners of unlawful acts, ensure good order and discipline among prisoners, attend to their wellbeing and to give effect to any directions as to the prisoners' treatment which are given by a court (section 104(3)). Reasonable force may be used by the officer in the execution of his duties (section 104(5)). Breaches of discipline by a prisoner under the control of a custody officer on escort duties may be dealt with by the governor of the receiving prison or the director of a contracted out prison (section 105). Prison custody officers generally have the same powers as prison officers, but, except when acting under an escort arrangement or in a contracted out prison, are not authorised to search persons in or seeking to enter any prison who are suspected of possessing any prohibited article (section 108). Any person who is, or has been, employed in the performance of any escort function, at a contracted out prison or in the performance of a contracted out function at a directly managed prison, commits an offence if he reveals, other than in the course of duty or as authorised by the Secretary of State, any information acquired in the course of duty applying to an individual prisoner (section 115).

CHAPTER 4

THE REGULATION OF DAILY LIFE IN PRISON

Where previously many of the details regulating daily life in **04–01** the prison were governed by standing orders, the situation since the enactment of the Prisons and Young Offenders Institutions (Scotland) Rules 1994 is much more open and easier to describe. It is also suggested that the form of the new Rules materially affects their justiciability (see the argument above in Chapter 3). In particular, there has been a departure from the notion that prisoners only have privileges, which can be taken away in circumstances as defined by the grantor, and a distinct move towards according certain things as rights. Thus the Rules require that the governor of each prison shall establish a system of privileges for the establishment and detail, *inter alia*, the circumstances in which these privileges may be withdrawn from a prisoner (rule 40(1)). Rule 40(4) explicitly distinguishes such privileges from any entitlement or right of a prisoner specified in any other provision of the Rules: "and any such entitlement or right shall not be regarded as a privilege granted by virtue of this rule and shall not be capable of being forfeited under rule 100(1)(b)" (the provision allowing a governor to award forfeiture of privileges as a disciplinary punishment). Accordingly, it is now possible to describe many of the provisions regulating the daily life of prisoners as rights, and it may be that these provisions will be directly enforceable through court action when the provisions of the Rules are not followed.

For the purposes of presentation, the main provisions **04–02** governing daily life in prison are presented alphabetically. The text generally describes the situation of convicted and sentenced adult male prisoners. Where there are differences in relation to unconvicted, unsentenced appellants (including those whose sentence is being appealed by the Crown), civil prisoners, female prisoners, immigration detainees and young prisoners, these are considered in separate paragraphs at the end of this chapter. The complaints and discipline provisions within prisons are dealt with separately in Chapter 5 and legal enforcement measures are discussed in Chapter 6.

Accommodation

04–03   Prisoners are entitled to accommodation in a single cell or room except where the nature of accommodation in a prison or the circumstances pertaining in that prison or any other prison to which the Prison (Scotland) Rules apply make it necessary for the prisoner to share a cell or room, or the governor or medical officer considers it desirable that a particular prisoner share a room or cell. If a room or cell is used to accommodate more than one person, they will be chosen by the governor or medical officer as suitable to share with each other (rule 15(3)). Thus cell sharing can be ordered because of overcrowding, but the previous rule requiring that the minimum number of people in shared accommodation should be three has been abandoned.

04–04   Each cell or room used for the accommodation of prisoners must be fitted with a means of communicating with an officer (rule 16(1)). All parts of a prison to which prisoners have access, including their cells or rooms, are required to be of an adequate size and to be heated, lighted, ventilated and furnished as is necessary for the health and safety of prisoners (rule 16(2)). No definition of "adequate" in relation to any of these factors is given in the Rules. It might therefore be difficult to challenge any particular decision to use a cell or room for the accommodation of a number of prisoners, but it seems likely that standards specifying minimum space for each prisoner in a cell will be developed by international bodies involved in penal affairs, and it may be that such standards could be used as a literal yard-stick in a domestic challenge. (See further below, Chapter 7.)

Age

04–05   Persons under the age of 21 sentenced to detention must normally be kept in a young offenders institution (1989 Act, section 20A). The Secretary of State may, however, provide by direction that such a person be kept in a prison or remand centre, though, if the person is younger than 18, only for a limited purpose (*ibid.*, section 20A(2)). A person may be kept in a young offenders institution after the age of 21, but must be transferred to a prison at the latest on the day before his 23rd birthday (*ibid.*, section 21).

Allocation

Section 10 of the 1989 Act, as substituted by section 22 of the **04–06** 1993 Act, allows the Secretary of State to commit any prisoner to any prison and to move a prisoner at any time to any other prison. Rule 13 authorises the Secretary of State to set aside prisons or particular parts of them for particular classes of prisoner or for particular purposes; subject to this, governors may allocate within their prisons any particular part within which a prisoner or class of prisoners may be confined, having regard to the classification of the prisoner, the security category of the prisoner and any other matter affecting the management of the prisoner (rule 13(2)). The governor must, at the request of a prisoner, provide an explanation as to why the prisoner has been allocated to a particular part of a prison (rule 13(3)).

Accordingly, there appears to be a wide discretion in **04–07** terms of not only to which prison but also where within any prison a prisoner may be allocated. In the case of *Thomson, Petitioner*, 1989 S.L.T. 343, a prisoner sought judicial review of a decision to transfer him from Glenochil prison to Peterhead. It was held that judicial review was available in such matters, but the court said that it would only be in "rare and exceptional" circumstances that it would intervene (at page 345B), and that it would be necessary to find that the Secretary of State had acted illegally in the process. The main allegation which had been made in the *Thomson* case was that the prisoner had not been informed of the reasons for the decision. The court held that prisoners had no right to know the basis on which a transfer decision had been made, and accordingly there was no breach of the law. It may be that this case was argued on the wrong basis. The petitioner had also been regraded from security category C to B on his prison transfer, but no argument was presented to the court on the significance of this. It may be that now that the security categories are fully in the public domain in the 1994 Rules, and that the system of privileges at each prison is public knowledge, the argument could be greatly elaborated (See further, McManus, *"Prisoners' Rights in Scotland: Judicial Review of Allocation Decisions"*, 149 SCOLAG 25). Nonetheless, it presumably remains the case that Scottish courts will be reluctant to intervene in allocation decisions given the very wide discretion which both the Act and the Rules accord to the Secretary of State.

04–08   *Opportunity and Responsibility* indicates an intention on the part of the SPS to allow prisoners, as far as possible, to choose the prison in which they wish to serve their sentence. Pressure of numbers on available space, as well as security and related considerations, have so far created difficulties in this regard, but some progress has been made. Thus, most short-term adult male convicted persons can now serve their sentence in their local prison, which is what opinion surveys of prisoners indicate is their commonest desire (to facilitate family visits). The limited accommodation for female prisoners and young offenders renders this more difficult for these groups. Equally, specialist facilities—for example for the treatment of sex offenders—cannot economically be provided in every prison and are thus concentrated in particular establishments. There will always, therefore, be some need to locate prisoners in prisons other than the ones they might choose, and the law leaves a wide discretion to the Secretary of State in this matter.

Association and Removal Therefrom

04–09   The rules give no positive right to prisoners to associate with each other during their imprisonment, but such a right can be implied from the fact that removal from association can only be authorised in four particular sets of circumstances.

04–10   *First*, rule 80(1) empowers a governor, when he considers it desirable for the purpose of maintaining good order or discipline, protecting the interests of any prisoner, or ensuring the safety of any other persons, to arrange for the removal of a prisoner from association either generally or for any particular purposes. The governor must specify in the order the reasons why he is making it and must explain these reasons to the prisoner (rule 80(4)). Only with the authority of the Secretary of State may removal from general association last for more than 72 hours (rule 80(5)), and each such authority can be for a maximum of one month, though this may be renewed from month to month (rule 80(6)). Removal from association in relation to particular activities is also subject to a limit of 72 hours, but the governor may make a further order in relation to the same activities which must then be reviewed on a weekly basis thereafter (rule 80(7)). The governor retains discretion to remove this restriction at any time and must do so if the medical officer so advises on medical grounds (rule 80(7)). If a prisoner under such an order is transferred to another prison, any order automatically lapses, but the governor of the receiving prisoner may also exercise the power to make a new order (rule 80(9)).

Secondly, rule 85 permits the governor to order the temporary confinement in a special cell of a prisoner who is refractory, or acting in a violent manner (rule 85(1)). No prisoner may be so detained as a punishment or for longer than 24 hours (rule 85(2)). All particulars of such confinements must be recorded and the medical officer must be informed of them as soon as possible (rule 85(3)). The medical officer must visit any prisoner who has been so confined for a continuous period in excess of 15 hours, and all such prisoners must be visited by an officer at least every 15 minutes during the confinement (rule 85(4)).

04–11

Thirdly, cellular confinement of any prisoner over the age of 16 can be ordered as a punishment under rule 100(1)(d) for a maximum period of three days. This period cannot be extended by consecutive awards imposed at the same time for more than one offence arising from the same incident (rule 100(3)). If this punishment is awarded, the medical officer must be informed as soon as possible (rule 100(6)). By direction made under rule 100(6), persons subject to cellular confinement must be provided with basic furniture and access to sanitary facilities, and may be allowed to keep such items of property as are compatible with such confinement. They are not to be allowed to have cash or to purchase articles in prison except replacement batteries, phone cards or postage stamps.

04–12

Fourthly, a governor may order that a prisoner who has been reported for an alleged disciplinary offence be removed from association with other prisoners until adjudication of the breach of discipline (rule 95(2)). Such a removal cannot exceed 72 hours except in exceptional circumstances and with the written authority of the Secretary of State (rule 92(3)(4)).

04–13

Accordingly, removal from association is available for a variety of reasons, each with its own restrictions. It remains possible for a prisoner to request to be kept apart from other prisoners—for example when he fears for his own safety if kept in association—but this now appears to require the authority of the Secretary of State under rule 80. A practice has developed in some prisons of placing prisoners in

04–14

"limited association" for control purposes. In this type of regime prisoners are allowed to associate in small numbers at exercise and recreation, but may be kept in their cells for considerably longer than the normal regime in the rest of the prison. The legal basis for this was not clear under the old rules, and continues to be questionable under the new rules, which make no provision for this halfway house. Presumably, a governor could exercise his power under rule 40 to provide for different privileges, including different amounts of time out of cell for recreational and other purposes for different classes of prisoner. But rule 11 does not allow behaviour of prisoners as a factor to be taken into account in their classification. It would be possible under rule 13 for the governor to allocate a particular part of the prison for the holding of troublesome prisoners, but it is suggested that, in the absence of an explicit power within this rule to limit association, any such limitation would be challengeable by prisoners subjected to it.

Business Activity by Prisoners

04–15 The Act is silent on this matter, but the Rules take it upon themselves to issue a general prohibition on all convicted prisoners carrying on any trade, profession or vocation from the prison (rule 77(1)). A prisoner may, however, take such steps as are necessary to protect the value of any interest he may have in any property or business (rule 77(2)(a)) and may also write articles or books for publication (whether or not in a professional capacity), insofar as this is compatible with the Rules, any direction made under the Rules, and the prison regime in general (rule 77(2)(b)). It is difficult to see the logic in these provisions.

Counselling

04–16 Governors may arrange such counselling programmes as they consider appropriate to the needs of prisoners, and attendance at counselling may be treated as an activity in lieu of work (rule 73(2)). Most establishments have some form of counselling in relation to alcohol and drugs problems, in addition to regular counselling provided by social workers and psychologists within the prison. There is, however, no entitlement to counselling.

Classification and Security Categories

Governors may classify prisoners in accordance with the following factors: age, sex, offence or matter in respect of which the person is committed to custody, period of sentence, or committal and previous record (rule 11). In addition, governors must assign each prisoner to a security category as soon as possible after reception (rule 12(1)).   **04–17**

Security categories are defined in Schedule 2 to the rules. They are: **04–18**

Category A: A prisoner who would place national security at risk, or be highly dangerous to the public, or to prison staff and their families, or to the police in the event of an escape, and who must be kept in conditions of maximum security.

Category B: A prisoner who is considered likely to be a danger to the public, and who must be kept in secure conditions to prevent his escape.

Category C: A prisoner who is considered unlikely to be a danger to the public, and who can be given the opportunity to serve his sentence with the minimum of restrictions.

Category D: A prisoner who is considered not to be a danger to the public, and who can be given the opportunity to serve his sentence in open conditions.

The governor must allocate each prisoner to the lowest suitable category and keep the matter under review, with a minimum of a formal review each year (rule 12(2)(3)). Untried prisoners must be allocated to either category A or B, whichever is the lower appropriate, and may be moved from one to the other by the governor at any time (rule 12(4)(5)). In any case where a prisoner is allocated to category A, the governor must obtain the approval of the Secretary of State to this within 72 hours; equally, the prior approval of the   **04–19**

Secretary of State is required before any life sentence prisoner can be moved to category D (rule 12(6)(7)). At the request of the prisoner the governor must explain why he has allocated the prisoner to a particular security category and inform the prisoner of the gist of any matter of fact or opinion to which the governor has had regard in reaching the decision, subject to the protection of information likely to be damaging to the prisoner or any other person, and information likely to result in the commission of a crime, facilitate an escape, impede the prevention or detection of crime or otherwise damage the public interest (rule 12(8)(9)).

04–20 Security categories are a crucial determinant of many of the conditions of imprisonment to which a prisoner is subjected. The allocation process is thus very important. Where previously this was a matter regulated by standing orders, the incorporation of the categories and the criteria for allocation to them in the Rules, and the requirement that reasons be given, may render the issue more open to legal challenge. The SPS has made a commitment, in *Custody and Care*, to ensure that prisoners are allocated to the lowest appropriate category, and the Rules reflect this. Clearly, many of the matters to be taken into account in making allocations to categories are properly security considerations. The courts might therefore be reluctant to intervene, but there is a strong case for ensuring that the *system* of allocation works in accordance with the requirements of natural justice. One unreported English case, while security categories were a matter for standing orders in England, supports this proposition (*Payne* v. *Home Office*, May 2, 1977, unreported), but the European Court of Human Rights has made it clear that this is not a matter regulated by the Convention (*Brady* v. *U.K.* (1979) 3 E.H.R.R. 297).

Clothing

04–21 On their face, the new Rules depart radically from the old in providing that all prisoners may wear their own clothes (rule 18(1)). However, the same rule provides that the Secretary of State may, by direction, exclude the operation of this rule in particular prisons or parts of prisons and a direction has been issued which excludes the rule in all but open prisons. Accordingly, it continues to be the exception which governs.

Even then, the right to wear own clothes is not an absolute **04–22**
one. Particular clothing may be ordered to be worn for legal
proceedings, or by the medical officer for the purposes of
health or on medical grounds (rule 18(2)(a)(b)). In addition,
the governor may decide that the prisoner's clothing is in
poor condition, may be prejudicial to security, good order or
discipline within the prison, or is incompatible with the
facilities at or management of the prison, and order that the
prisoner wear alternative clothing (rule 18(2)(c)). Special or
protective clothing may also be ordered for particular work
or other activities undertaken by the prisoner, and a
governor can order the forfeiture of the right to wear own
clothing as a disciplinary award under rule 100 (see below)
(rule 18(2)(d)(e)).

Any prisoner who is not allowed, or who chooses not, to **04–23**
wear his own clothing must be supplied with suitable
clothing by the Secretary of State (rule 19(1)). "Suitable" is
defined as meaning clothing which is of good condition,
appearance and fit and, in the circumstances, suitable for the
health and safety of the prisoner (rule 19(2)). As far as
practicable, officially issued clothing should be for the
personal use of one prisoner, must be maintained in good
repair and, if required to be worn by the prisoner outwith the
prison, should not give any indication that the person is a
prisoner (rule 19(3)(c)).

Governors are obliged to ensure that every prisoner has **04–24**
sufficient clothing to enable him to change daily his socks,
underwear and whatever other items the Secretary of State
may specify in a direction, and to have a clean change of
other clothing as is necessary for the purposes of health and
hygiene (rule 20(1)). If this is not practicable for any reasons
relating to the circumstances of facilities in a particular
prison, the Secretary of State may, by direction, exclude the
application of this rule in that prison (rule 12(2)). The only
direction made immediately on the coming into force of the
Rules is one in relation to Polmont Young Offenders
Institution, where changes of basic clothing are to be allowed
five times per week.

These provisions relating to clothing are all a considerable **04–25**
improvement on the previous position. Many prisons only
allowed twice weekly changes of underclothing and socks.
Stocks of clothing, as well as laundry arrangements, will
require to be improved considerably to ensure that the new
requirements can be met.

Death of a Prisoner

04–26   Governors are obliged to give immediate notification of the death of a prisoner to the procurator fiscal, the visiting committee and, where practicable, to the nearest relative of the prisoner (1989 Act, section 34). A public inquiry must be held into the death of any person in legal custody (Fatal Accidents and Sudden Deaths Inquiry (Scotland) Act 1976, sections 1(1)(a)(ii)).

Drug Testing

04–27   The 1994 Act amends the 1989 Act to allow rules to be made requiring any prisoner confined in a prison for which an authorisation is in force to provide a sample of urine for the purposes of determining whether the prisoner has any drug in his body. The authorisation may also extend to requiring the prisoner to provide any other non-intimate sample instead of or in addition to a urine sample. "Drug" is defined as any controlled drug for the purposes of the Misuse of Drugs Act 1971, and "intimate samples" are samples of blood, semen or any other tissue fluid, saliva or pubic hair, or a swab taken from a person's body orifice. (1989 Act, section 41B, as inserted by 1994 Act, section 151(2)).

Education

04–28   Prisoners under the normal minimum school leaving age must be provided with education in accordance with the Education Acts. For all other prisoners, governors are obliged to arrange a programme of educational classes suitable, as far as practicable, to the interests and needs of prisoners (rule 72(1)). A prisoner may be allowed to undertake an educational class in lieu of the requirement to work (rule 72(2)), and continue to receive remuneration while doing so at rates to be specified in a direction by the Secretary of State (rule 74). The direction specifies that the rate of pay shall be the same as the prisoner was previously earning in the week in which he last undertook work.

04–29   Most penal establishments have a varied educational programme, involving classes in basic literacy, courses leading to recognised awards, up to and including Open

University degrees, and artistic and recreational pursuits. Attendance at all classes is voluntary for those over the minimum school leaving age, but there is often competition for the available spaces.

Exercise

Every prisoner is entitled to a minimum of one hour of exercise per day, out of doors (rule 75(1)). Such exercise must take place in association with other prisoners, unless a prisoner has been removed from association (see above, rule 80). The Secretary of State may remove this right, by direction, if he considers that it is not practicable because of "exceptional circumstances pertaining in a prison" to allow exercise (rule 75(3)). **04–30**

Food

Governors must ensure that each prisoner is supplied with sufficient wholesome and nutritious food and drink, well prepared and presented, which takes into account the prisoner's age, health and, so far as reasonably practicable, his religious, cultural or other requirements (rule 21(1)). There is thus no absolute entitlement to special religious or other diets, though there seems no reason why provision of the most common diets, especially vegetarian and vegan, should ever not be reasonably practicable. **04–31**

Governors are also obliged to ensure regular inspection of the quality and quantity of prisoners' food and drink, before and after preparation and at the point of delivery, and the conditions under which they are prepared, and to remedy any deficiency as soon as practicable (rule 21(3)(4)). Visiting committee members are also under a specific obligation to inspect the food and drink provided to prisoners (rule 135(a)). **04–32**

Only food provided within the prison or bought by the prisoner within the prison may be received by a prisoner, unless the governor or medical officer authorises otherwise (rule 21(5)). **04–33**

In exceptional circumstances, the Secretary of State may, by direction, exempt a governor from the duty to provide a prisoners with food in accordance with this rule (rule 21(2)). **04–34**

Like other such provisions in these Rules, this is simply to cover for disturbances and other events which would render compliance with the individual rule difficult or impossible.

Hygiene

04–35   Every prisoner must be provided with opportunities, and such toilet articles as are necessary, for health and cleanliness (rule 22(1)). Access to facilities for washing and bathing or showering must be provided at all reasonable times, with a minimum provision of two baths or showers per week (rule 22(1)). Prisoners are entitled to grow facial hair and to keep their hair at such length as they wish, unless the medical officer orders otherwise on medical grounds (rule 22(3)).

04–36   Prisoners' bedding must also be changed as frequently as necessary to ensure cleanliness (rule 17(2)), and prisoners must keep their cells or rooms in a clean and tidy condition, unless exempted by the medical officer for medical reasons, or the governor for any other reason (rule 16(3)).

Information to Prisoners

04–37   The Prison Rules and any directions made under them must be made readily available to all prisoners (rule 5). In addition, on reception into a prison for the first time other than on transfer from another prison, a prisoner is entitled to the following:

> information on, and reasonable facilities for, contacting up to two persons and a legal adviser to tell them about his admission to prison;
> if the prisoner is a foreign national, an additional opportunity to contact a diplomatic representative of his choice;
> if the prisoner is a stateless person or a refugee, an opportunity to contact a diplomatic representative of any state which may look after his interest and any national or international organisation whose purpose is to serve the interests of refugees or stateless persons or to protect their civil rights;
> if the person is committed to prison in default of

payment of a sum of money, information on the facilities available for arranging such payment as would secure his release from custody;

information in writing, for all prisoners, on the rules, directions and standing orders which apply in the particular prison, the prison routine and regime, how to make requests and complaints, how contact with friends and relatives may be maintained, and any right of appeal against conviction and/or sentence available under the Criminal Procedure (Scotland) Act 1975 or the relevant statute governing courts martial appeals;

where the prisoner's release date can be calculated, he should be told what it is as soon as reasonably practicable (rule 9).

On subsequent transfer to another prison, the prisoner **04–38** must be informed of the local rules pertaining to its regime. Any information required to be provided under this rule must be provided in a manner which enables the prisoner to understand it (rule 9(8)).

Legalised Police Cells

In addition to the established prisons in Scotland, the 1989 **04–39** Act continues a provision enabling police cells to be designated as prisons by rules under the Act (section 14). Such cells, 22 of which are currently licensed under the Act, may be used for the accommodation of prisoners before, during or after trial for a period not exceeding 30 days (section 14(1)). Legalised police cells are governed by the Prison (Scotland) Rules 1994. In practice, many legalised police cells are rarely used, with only Campbeltown, Hawick, Kirkwall, Lochmaddy, Oban, Stornoway and Thurso being used at all in 1992 and none of these reaching an average daily occupancy of one in 1992 (SPS Annual Report, 1992, Appendix 1). In his foreword to the annual report of HMCIP for 1992–93 (1993, Cm. 2348), the Secretary of State observed that the need to appoint visiting committees to the legalised police cells was under discussion between the SPS and its legal advisers.

Letters

04–40   This is the area in which the greatest number of changes have been forced on prison regulations by cases decided before the European Court of Human Rights. A whole series of cases, starting with *Golder* v. *U.K.* (1975) 1 E.H.R.R. 524, has challenged the original provisions which made all letters subject to censorship, limited the category of person to whom a prisoner could write, and permitted the prison authorities to stop letters, or parts of them which were considered objectionable. After a period of piecemeal changes to comply with these judgments, the Rules have been completely redrafted. The current provisions are as follows:

1. General Right to Send or Receive Letters and Packets

04–41   A prisoner has a general right, subject to the restrictions mentioned below, to send and receive letters and postal packages by means of the postal services or otherwise (rule 48). Prisoners are entitled to be supplied with materials for writing one letter per week and postage on this letter is to be paid by the Secretary of State (rule 53(1) and (2)). The governor may allow such other letters at public expense as he considers appropriate (rule 53(3)).

2. Letters or Postal Packets to or from Courts

04–42   No such correspondence shall be opened or read by prison authorities except where an officer has cause to believe that it contains a prohibited article, and has explained this cause to the prisoner, when the officer may open, but not read, the correspondence, only in the presence of the prisoner (rule 49(1)–(5)). The governor may confiscate any prohibited article found (rule 49(6)). The term "court" is defined as including the European Court of Justice, the European Court of Human Rights, the European Commission of Human Rights and the Parole Board for Scotland (rule 49(7)).

3. Correspondence to and from Legal Advisers

04–43   Again, such correspondence can only be opened by an officer when he has cause to believe that it contains a prohibited article and explains the reasons for this belief to the prisoner when the prisoner is present (rule 50(1)–(4)). In addition, however, such correspondence may be read by an officer where the governor has cause to believe that the contents endanger the security of the prison or the safety of any person, or relate to a criminal activity (rule 50(6)). If a letter is to be read, the prisoner must be informed and given reasons, and the letter may only be read by the governor or an officer specially authorised by him (rule 50(7)).

4. Any Other Correspondence

Any other letter or postal packet sent to or by a prisoner may **04–44** be opened by an officer (rule 51(1)). Correspondence may only be read when an officer considers that it contains material forbidden by the directions made under rule 52 (rule 51(2)). The directions provide that all the mail sent to or by a category A prisoner should be read by an authorised officer; in relation to other categories of prisoner, mail should only be read where the authorised officer believes that it contains material likely to be prejudicial to the good order or security of the prison, or relating to a criminal activity. If anything contravening the restrictions is found, the officer may prevent the letter or packet, or anything in it, being sent or received by the prisoner, and dispose of the offending item in accordance with provisions in the directions (rule 51(3)). The directions made under this rule require the governor to return any inappropriate letter or package to the sender, if known, and to inform the prisoner and record details on the prisoner's file. In relation to outgoing mail, it should be returned to the prisoner with an explanation of why it is not to be sent, and the details should be recorded on the prisoner's file.

The rule also provides that the directions should contain **04–45** any restrictions which may be imposed on the number of letters and packets the prisoner may send and receive, the range of addressees to whom they may be sent and the type, category or nature of such letters and packets (rule 52). The previous position in Scotland has been that prisoners are generally allowed one letter per week at public expense and as many others as they wish to pay for. No restrictions have been imposed on the number of incoming letters. The directions provide that the amount of outgoing mail from convicted prisoners is to be limited only by their ability to pay the postage from prison earnings; addressees are unrestricted except that mail sent to persons other than a spouse of the prisoner, who have notified the governor in writing that they do not wish to receive mail from the prisoner, may be withheld, as may communications to persons, other than close relatives of the prisoner, or organisations whom the governor has reasonable grounds for suspecting may be planning or involved in activities which constitute a genuine threat to the security and good order of the prison.

Marriage

04–46   The Act and the Rules are silent on the question of whether prisoners may marry during a period of confinement. However, the European Court of Human Rights has held that there is no justification for restricting the right of prisoners to undergo a marriage ceremony (*Hamer* v. *U.K.* (1982) 4 E.H.R.R. 139), and it has not been the recent practice in Scotland to limit this right. It may be, of course, that permission to go outside the prison in order to attend the ceremony is refused, but, given that Scots law allows marriages to be conducted anywhere, it is possible to arrange for the ceremony to be held within the prison. There is no right to consummate the marriage during the period of imprisonment.

Medical and Dental Treatment

04–47   The Secretary of State is obliged to make such provision for medical and dental care of prisoners at each prison as he considers necessary (rule 24). The level of provision to the individual prisoner is at the discretion of the medical officer (rule 25), but the governor or other officer is under an obligation to bring to the attention of the medical officer any prisoner whose physical or mental condition appears to require the medical officer's attention (rule 26). Treatment, including any reference to specialists, transfer to an outside hospital and medication, is at the discretion of the medical officer (rule 27). Prisoners are not entitled to second opinions, or to be treated by a doctor of their own choosing. If a prisoner becomes seriously ill, sustains a serious injury or is transferred to an outside hospital, the governor is under an obligation to inform a relative or friend of the prisoner, or such other person as the governor considers appropriate, unless the prisoner has requested otherwise (rule 30). Different provisions apply to untried and civil prisoners, who may be visited by medical and dental practitioners of their own choice, provided that the prisoner takes responsibility for the payment of any expenses involved (rule 34).

News and Current Affairs

Prisoners must be allowed to keep themselves informed of **04–48** current affairs through books, neswspapers, periodicals, radio or any other medium the governor may allow, with restrictions and conditions imposed by the governor only when necessary to protect the prisoner from self-injury, or to prevent the prisoner from injuring others (rule 47). It has been the practice in the past for prisoners to be allowed to receive any newspaper or periodical as long as it is sent directly to the prison from a recognised newsagent, and this is continued in rule 46. Payment may be made by the prisoner or a person outwith the prison, and the materials will be subject only to the same restrictions as apply to other incoming mail (see above).

Political Activity

1. Voting

Convicted prisoners are not allowed to vote (Representation **04–49** of the People Act 1983, section 3). Unconvicted prisoners— that is, remand and civil prisoners—are not disenfranchised, but it may be difficult to make arrangements to allow them to exercise this right, especially when they are received into prison shortly before an election is to take place.

2. Standing as a Candidate

Persons sentenced to imprisonment for a period of one year **04–50** or more are disqualified from membership of the House of Commons during that sentence (Representation of the People Act 1981, section 1). The seat of any M.P. so sentenced falls vacant on sentence and any nomination or election of a person serving one year or more would be void (*ibid.*, section 2).

Privileges

04–51 Each governor must establish such a system of privileges as may be appropriate to the class or classes of prisoners detained in the prison, and these privileges may apply to different classes of prisoner or different parts of the prison (rule 40). Matters to be covered in the system of privileges must, in terms of rule 40, include:

> items of property which a prisoner may keep in his cell;
> arrangements whereby a prisoner may purchase items within or outwith the prison;
> facilities to which a prisoner may have access and the activities in which he may take part;
> the arrangements whereby a prisoner may smoke or have any tobacco in his possession;
> the circumstances in which privileges may be withdrawn from a prisoner;
> any other matter specified in directions relating to this rule.

04–52 All privileges may be forfeited as a disciplinary measure under rule 100(1)(b), but the system of privileges must not prejudice or derogate from any entitlement or right of a prisoner under other rules, or render such entitlements or rights subject to forfeiture as a disciplinary award (rule 40(4)). Governors must ensure that every prisoner is informed in a way he can understand of what system of privileges is in force and the cirumstances in which each can be withdrawn (rule 40(5)).

Protection

04–53 The prison authorities have a common law duty of care towards prisoners, which may be breached, for example, when the authorities fail to prevent a foreseeable attack on a prisoner by another prisoner (*Whannel* v. *Secretary of State for Scotland*, 1989 S.L.T. 671). There is no public policy defence against such an action in Scotland (*Downie* v. *Secretary of State for Scotland and Chief Constable, Central Scotland Police*, 1989

S.C.L.R. 129), but the action must be based on the common law principles of negligence. Thus it is suggested that the English case of *Knight* v. *Home Office* [1990] 3 All E.R. 237, where it was held that the standard of care provided for a prisoner, who committed suicide in the prison hospital while awaiting transfer to a psychiatric hospital, was not required to be as high as the standard expected in an outside hospital, would be followed in Scotland.

The rules make no explicit provision for prisoners seeking   **04–54** special protection from other prisoners. However, governors are authorised to keep prisoners apart from each other to protect the prisoners' own interests, or to ensure the safety of other persons (rule 80(1)(b)(c)). Given that it is well known that certain categories of prisoner are likely to be at special risk if kept in normal association, it may be prima facie negligent for the authorities not to provide separate accommodation and facilities for such prisoners. Most Scottish prisons do make such provision available.

Prisoners' Property and Money

On reception into prison, every prisoner is searched and   **04–55** property which is prohibited removed from him (rule 7). Any prohibited article may be given to the police, and any medicines may be given to the prison medical officer (*ibid.*). All property brought with a prisoner or subsequently acquired by him must be recorded in an inventory, which the prisoner must be given an opportunity to check before signing it (rule 42). This requirement does not apply to property purchased within the prison, letters or other communications, and perishable or consumable goods (*ibid.*). The rules provide that the Secretary of State may provide, by a direction, what property a prisoner may keep in his cell, but in addition a governor may allow such other property as is compatible with the size and furnishings of the cell, health, safety, good order and such other matters as the governor considers relevant (rule 44). The current direction provides for a "reasonable" supply of toiletries, a number of photographs, a supply of pens, pencils and writing materials, a supply of other items which can be purchased from the prison canteen, and an amount of reading material. The governor must arrange for any property other than that which a prisoner is allowed to keep in his cell to be stored (rule 43). The governor, after notifying the prisoner, shall arrange for the disposal or destruction of anything which he considers to be prejudicial to health, safety, security or good order, unless the prisoner can arrange for its disposal (rule 43(2)).

04–56   Governors are empowered to specify whether prisoners, or any category of prisoner, may have cash in their possession and, if so, the maximum amount of such cash and the denominations in which it can be held (rule 45(1)). Any cash in excess of that allowed in possession shall be held by the governor on behalf of the prisoner, who may authorise the governor to deduct such sums as may be necessary for authorised purposes (rule 45(2)(3)). The governor may specify the maximum amount which can be so spent in any period, and the purposes for which it may be spent (rule 45(4)). A record of money held and spent must be kept in regard of each prisoner (rule 45(5)). Nothing in the Rules prevents a prisoner from opening or maintaining a bank or building society account, though the use of the account is subject to the Rules (Rule 45(6)).

Recreation

04–57   Governors are obliged to provide reasonable facilities and opportunities to enable prisoners to participate in recreational activities outwith normal working hours, though the only specific provision which must be made is a library (rule 76).

Release

04–58   Release dates for prisoners are calculated as explained in Chapter 6. Before release, the governor must discuss with the prisoner his immediate needs on release, and the governor may arrange for any other person to see the prisoner for this purpose (rule 117). The medical officer is also obliged to see any prisoner undergoing treatment or under his supervision before release, and certify that the prisoner is fit to travel (rule 118). No prisoner can be kept beyond his release date purely on medical grounds without his consent (*ibid.*). Prisoners are entitled to the return of all clothing and other property belonging to them on release and, if a prisoner has insufficient clothing of his own, the governor is obliged to provide suitable clothing for the prisoner's immediate needs on release (rule 119). Prisoners who are released from a prison outwith the district or islands area in which they were convicted are entitled to be taken back to the district or area of conviction at the expense of the Secretary of State (1989 Act, section 16(2)). The Secretary of State may also arrange for other prisoners to be conveyed to their homes, by paying their fares or by such other means as he may determine (section 17(1)), and may arrange payments to prisoners on release as, with the consent of the Treasury, he determines (section 17(2)). Practice has been that all prisoners (other than fine defaulters, civil prisoners and those awaiting deportation), serving more than 14 days are paid such sums as they would qualify for under normal income support regulations. Persons who would not qualify for income support (for example, because they have resources exceeding £8,000) do not qualify for this grant. Persons with no fixed abode on release qualify for a higher rate of grant. Any prisoner who does not receive a grant on release is given a subsistence allowance to cover the period until income support or a social fund loan can be obtained. Discharge grants are not taken into account in assessing entitlement to income support, though they may disqualify the ex-prisoner from a social fund loan. Provided they apply within seven days of release, ex-prisoners are entitled to income support from the day of release.

Religion

All prisoners must, as far as practicable, be allowed to observe the requirements of their religious and moral beliefs (rule 35), and the governor must ensure that they are made aware of the facilities and arrangements which exist for this purpose (*ibid.*). No prisoner may be visited against his will by any minister other than the Church of Scotland chaplain (1989 Act, section 9(4)). The Rules now recognise the existence of chaplaincy teams and impose on each member of the team an obligation to visit prisoners of their own denomination as soon as possible after admission and to organise services, meetings and such other arrangements as are necessary, with the approval of, or in consultation with, the governor (rule 36(1)). Any person may, with the approval   **04–59** of the governor, act on behalf of the chaplaincy team in the member's absence or assist the member in carrying out any of their duties (rule 36(2)). All prisoners belonging to a religious denomination are entitled to attend services or meetings of that denomination as arranged in the prison save when the governor considers, in exceptional circumstances, that this would be prejudicial to the interests of good order (rule 38(1)(2)). The governor must also notify the chaplain or visiting minister as soon as practicable of any request by a prisoner to receive a visit from him, and any visits to prisoners by members of the chaplaincy team are to be held outwith the sight and hearing of an officer unless the member requests otherwise or the governor considers that it would be prejudicial to the interests of security or to the safety of the member (rule 38(3)(4)). Prisoners must be provided with books, literature and other materials, as the governor considers appropriate, for their religious needs, and may keep in their possession appropriate materials (rule 39). Prisoners who have declared themselves to be of a particular religious denomination are entitled, when it is reasonably practicable having regard to the requirements of the prison regime, to take their rest day from work or study on the recognised day of religious observance for that denomination, and to be excused work or classes on such other recognised days of observance for that denomination as the Secretary of State may, by direction, specify (rule 69(3)). The former restrictions on a prisoner's freedom to change his religious denomination are absent from the new Rules.

Restraints

04–60   The only restraint authorised by the Rules is a body belt (rule 83(1)). Its use may be authorised by the governor, to prevent the prisoner injuring himself or others, or from damaging property, creating a disturbance, or escaping from safe custody during transfer, or by the medical officer, only to prevent self-injury (rule 83(2)(5)). When either authorises the use of a restraint, they must immediately notify the other, and the medical officer can order the removal of any restraint authorised by the governor (rule 83(3)(6)(4)). Restraints must not be used as a punishment (rule 83(7)).

Restraints cannot be used for longer than 24 hours without **04–61** the authority of the Secretary of State, and must, in any case, be removed as soon as possible (rule 84(1)). Directions will provide the method of application of each restraint, and the circumstances in which they must be temporarily removed (rule 84(3)). While under restraint, prisoners must be visited at least every 15 minutes by an officer (rule 84(4)), must be examined by a medical officer immediately after the restraint is imposed and after it is removed (rule 84(5)), and the governor must record all particulars of use of restraints and give notice to the Secretary of State of the particulars forthwith (rule 84(6)).

Both body belts and loose canvas restraint jackets (strait **04–62** jackets) have been available for use in penal establishments until recent times. Advances in staff training in methods of control and restraint have rendered strait jackets practically obsolete, and their use is thus no longer authorised.

Searching

Prisoners may be searched at any time, and will be searched **04–63** on reception into a prison (rules 7(1), 88). Searches may take the form of an examination of a prisoner's person and clothing without the prisoner undressing, the removal and examination of a prisoner's clothing, the visual examination of the external parts of a prisoner's body after the removal of clothing or, if the prisoner consents, the visual examination of his open mouth without the use of force or any instrument (rule 88(2)). There is now power under this rule authorising the physical examination of a prisoner's orifices (rule 88(5)). Searches may only be carried out by an officer of the same sex as the prisoner, and must be done as expeditiously and decently as possible (rule 88(3)). Any search involving removal of clothing must be carried out by two officers of the same sex and outwith the sight of any other prisoner (*ibid.*). Other conditions may be laid down by the Secretary of State in directions (*ibid.*). A prisoner may be searched at such times and in such circumstances as the governor considers necessary (rule 88(4)). Any item of property belonging to a prisoner may be searched by an officer at any time, and the room or cell of any prisoner shall be searched at such times as the governor considers necessary (rule 89).

04–64   There is thus a wide discretion as to the frequency with which searches may be carried out. However, it is clear that invasive searching by prison authorities is never authorised, though they may, of course, call the police if they feel that an illegal act has been committed which would require a search authorised by warrant.

Telephones

04–65   Prisoners may have access to telephones in accordance with rule 54 and directions made thereunder. The rule provides for limits to be put on the groups and categories of prisoner, the times of day, the circumstances in which and the conditions under which such access may be allowed, and provide for the logging, monitoring and recording by an officer of any calls a prisoner may make (*ibid.*). Any prisoner refused the use of a telephone must be told the reasons for this refusal (*ibid.*). The directions so far made enable all classes of prisoners to have access to card telephones, at times of day which vary from establishment to establishment depending on the routine of the establishment. The use of card phones can be withdrawn from individual prisoners or groups or categories of prisoner in the circumstances defined in the directive. Prisoners may make outgoing calls only and cannot telephone numbers beginning with the figures 1 or 0800, the number 999 or such other numbers as the governor may determine, to persons who have indicated in writing to the governor that they do not wish to receive calls from a particular prisoner or to persons to whom the prisoner may not write. Calls which are, in the opinion of the governor, mischievous, malicious or threatening, or constitute or form part of any criminal activity or attempted criminal activity may also be banned.

04–66   Use of a phone card by a prisoner is held to imply his consent to the logging, monitoring and recording of the call and to any interception in terms of the Interception of Communications Act 1985. In general, records of calls are to be destroyed after three months and recordings of any calls after 28 days. All calls made by category A prisoners are to be monitored and any other calls may be monitored. Prisoners are to be allowed to purchase a maximum of five phone cards per week from the prison canteen, but may be allowed extra cards for the purpose of making calls in relation to legal proceedings or in such other circumstances as the governor may consider reasonable.

Temporary Release

The Secretary of State is empowered to make a direction **04–67** governing the circumstances in which and the purposes for which temporary release may be authorised by a governor, the prisoners or classes of prisoners eligible for such release, and the conditions which a governor may impose on such releases (rule 126). Governors may then grant temporary release in accordance with the direction (rules 120–124). Any prisoner on temporary release is liable to be recalled to prison by order of the Secretary of State, whether the conditions of that temporary release have been broken or not (rule 125).

Opportunity and Responsibility made a commitment to **04–68** increasing the amount of home leaves available, with due regard to security and the safety of the public, as a method of enabling prisoners to keep in touch with their families and general conditions outside prisons. The new Rules make provision for six types of home leave: short home leave, Christmas and summer leave, pre-training for freedom leave, long home leave, pre-parole leave and unescorted exceptional day release. In all cases, prisoners must be in security category D, and have been for a minimum of six weeks, before they can qualify for home leave, and, in the case of the first four types of leave, must be located in a hall or prison to which these rules are applied by direction.

The relevant direction specifies that category D prisoners **04–69** in all prisons can be considered for the first four types of leave. Before granting any of these, however, the governor must check that the prisoner is eligible, obtain reports on his suitability for leave, obtain a report on the address at which the leave would be taken, consider the offence(s) for which the prisoner is serving the sentence and the attitude of the offender, the victim and the community to the offence(s), consider the stability of the offender's relationship with his family, and assess the risk that the prisoner may abscond and/or present a danger to the public. The governor's decision, with reasons, must be recorded in writing. The prisoner's conduct and industry in the prison must have been satisfactory in the six months prior to the leave.

Christmas and summer leaves are for a maximum of five days (excluding travelling time), and are only available to prisoners in open regimes. Pre-training for freedom leave is also for a maximum of five days. Short home leave is for a maximum of 48 hours (excluding travelling time), and is available every two weeks for prisoners on training for freedom, every four weeks for those in open regimes, and every eight weeks for all other category D prisoners.

04–70   Long home leave is only available to prisoners who are serving a sentence of more than one year and who still have at least two months of their sentence to run (rule 121). Otherwise, the same criteria must be satisfied as in relation to short home leaves. The leave may only be granted once, and must be taken within the two months before release but before the last seven days of the sentence. The leave allows a maximum of five days at the approved address, excluding travelling time.

04–71   Prisoners who are to be released on parole or life licence, and who have not had long home leave, are eligible for a period of three days home leave before their final release, providing all the usual conditions are met.

04–72   Finally, governors may grant unescorted exceptional day release, on the written application of the prisoner, to any category D prisoner, for the purpose of visiting a dangerously ill near relative, attending a funeral of such a relative, visiting a parent who is too old or too ill to travel to the prison, or for any other reason where the governor is of the opinion that there are exceptional circumstances (rule 123). Untried and civil prisoners cannot be considered for this privilege (*ibid.*).

04–73   Prisoners who are appellants, those subject to extradition and those considered by the medical officer to be mentally disordered or otherwise unfit are disqualified from consideration for home leaves (rule 124).

Tobacco

04–74   The possession and use of tobacco by convicted prisoners are privileges in terms of rule 40(3)(d). Untried and civil prisoners have, however, the right to possess tobacco, and to smoke at such times and in such places as the governor may allow (rule 41).

Transfer of Prisoners

Prisoners may be lawfully contained in any prison, and at **04–75**
any time moved from one prison to another by the Secretary
of State (1989 Act, section 10, as amended). (See also
Allocation, supra.) In addition, a prisoner may be transferred
to a mental hospital under the Mental Health (Scotland) Act
1984, subject to fulfilment of the conditions specified in that
Act (sections 71 and 73, rule 31). A prisoner being taken to or
from a prison must be exposed to public view as little as
possible and protected, as far as reasonably practicable, from
insult, curiosity and publicity in any form (rule 90(2)).
Prisoners who are allowed or required to be present in any
court must wear their own clothing or civilian clothing
supplied by the governor (rule 90(3)).

1. To Other Parts of the United Kingdom

Prisoners who come from, or have substantial links with, **04–76**
other parts of the U.K. may petition the Secretary of State for
transfer to a penal establishment in that other country.
Provided that both the Secretary of State and the Minister
responsible for the receiving country's prison system agree,
the prisoner may be transferred to serve the balance of the
sentence (Criminal Justice Act 1961, section 26). Difficulties
can arise in this regard because of different practices in
calculating release dates. The normal rule is that the date will
be determined under the system operating in the receiving
jurisdiction (section 26(4)). However, it was established in an
English case that it is a valid reason for refusal of transfer that
the system is more generous in the proposed receiving
country than in the sending country (*R.* v. *Secretary of State for
the Home Department ex p. McComb, The Times*, April 15, 1991).
On the other hand, in *Walsh* v. *Secretary of State for Scotland*,
1990 S.L.T. 526, it was held that a prisoner transferred from
England to Scotland under section 28(1) of the Criminal
Justice Act 1961 (permitting the compulsory transfer of
prisoners from one part of the U.K. to another for the
purposes of attending criminal proceedings against them),
retained the (then more generous) remission rights available
under the Rules applicable in England. Thus, if the transfer is
at the prisoner's own request, the system applicable in the
receiving jurisdiction will apply to him, but compulsory
transfers retain any rights available under the sending

country's Rules. The actual importance of this as between Scotland and England and Wales is less now that the release provisions are almost identical. It remains the case, however, that Northern Ireland has no parole system, but offers the possibility of half remission to all determinate sentence prisoners, and may thus appear attractive to some long-term prisoners.

2. To Other Countries

04–77   Under the Repatriation of Prisoners Act 1984 and the treaties negotiated with other countries which have accepted the convention for the transfer of sentenced persons, it may be possible for a foreign national to secure a transfer to his country of origin to serve his sentence. Both the receiving and the sending countries must be parties to the convention, and the Secretary of State and the appropriate authority in the other country must agree to the individual transfer. The prisoner's consent is also required. By no means all countries have accepted this right, a notable one being the Republic of Ireland.

Visits

1. By Persons of a Prisoner's Choice

04–78   Subject to the conditions explained below, each convicted prisoner is entitled to a visit either for not less than 30 minutes each seven consecutive days, or for not less than two hours in any period of 28 days (rule 55(2)). Prisoners under the age of 16 are entitled to a minimum of two visits of at least half an hour's duration each seven days (rule 55(3)). Untried and civil prisoners are allowed to receive a visit of at least 30 minutes' duration each day from Monday to Friday and, if a visit has not been taken on every day of the preceding Monday to Friday, a visit of at least 30 minutes on either Saturday or Sunday; governors also have discretion to allow further visits on a Saturday or Sunday of such duration as the governor thinks fit (rule 56). The number of visitors to be allowed at any one time is a matter for the governor's discretion (rule 55(4)). All visits must take place within the sight of an officer, but the officer must not listen to the conversation between a prisoner and his visitors unless the governor directs otherwise (rule 55(5)). The Secretary of State may, by direction, reduce this minimum entitlement when he considers that it is not practicable to allow it in view of the circumstances pertaining at any prison or the facilities available at it (rule 55(6)), and has directed that at Barlinnie prison the visit entitlement is to be one 30-minute visit on the day of admission and two 30-minute visits per calendar month thereafter. A governor may prohibit a visit by any person or terminate any such visit if he considers it necessary in the interests of security, discipline or the prevention of disorder or crime (rule 63). Prisoners may only receive visits from other prisoners in exceptional circumstances and with the permission of the governors of both prisons involved; a governor must give reasons for any refusal of such a visit (rule 55(7)). Further restrictions or conditions on visits may be imposed by means of directions, specifically relating to:

the use of video cameras for the recording of the visitors area during visits;
the introduction, possession or consumption of food or drink during visits;
the issuing of visit passes (rule 63(2)).

Directions so far issued permit the use of video recording equipment and microphones in any area where visits are taking place, allow only food and drink bought within the prison to be consumed during visits except in open establishments, Barlinnie special unit, Shotts alternative unit and Dumfries, and permit governors to institute a system of visit passes which specify the names of prisoner and visitors and the date of the visit. In relation to recording of visits, a notice must be prominently displayed informing visitors that this may be being used and prisoners and visitors are deemed to have given their consent to this being used.

Prisoners serving life sentences or sentences of more than **04–79** one year and who have served more than six months may be entitled to accumulate their visits entitlement and to carry any such entitlement forward to any other prison to which they may be transferred, subject to such directions as the Secretary of State may make (rule 57). The prisoner must have accumulated the equivalent of six month's visits entitlement (*ibid.*). Under the present directions, prisoners transferring between any of Barlinnie, Greenock, Edinburgh, Glenochil, Perth and Shotts prisons and between Glenochil and Polmont young offenders establishments cannot, save in exceptional circumstances, transfer visit entitlement.

Accumulated visits must be used within such a period as the governors may agree, and in any event within two months of transfer.

04–80 Visits normally take place in open surroundings with prisoners and visitors able to touch each other. However, the governor has power to order that any particular visit, or all visits to a particular prisoner, should take place in closed visit facilities where there is a barrier between prisoner and visitors (rule 64(1)). The circumstances in which the governor may make such an order are:

> where the governor is of the opinion that there are reasonable grounds for suspecting that the prisoner has previously obtained or is likely in the future to attempt to obtain any prohibited article from a visitor;
> the prisoner's behaviour makes it necessary for the purposes of security and control;
> any visit to the prisoner has been terminated due to the conduct of the visitor;
> a person who wishes to visit the prisoner has previously been refused entry to the prison; or
> the governor is of the opinion that this is necessary in relation to a visit allowed to an untried prisoner, an appellant, a civil prisoner, a remanded prisoner or a prisoner subject to a further charge or awaiting the outcome of a prosecution appeal against sentence in preparation of his case to ensure that it is necessary for this purpose (rule 64(2)).

04–81 Any such order in relation to closed visits must be reviewed at least every three months, and the order cannot be used as a disciplinary punishment (rule 64(3)(4)).

04–82 Visits provision has generally become much more liberal in Scotland in recent years. Most prisons can offer more than the minimum entitlement of visits, and the vast majority are held in open conditions. Closed visits are reserved for those who are considered to be a security risk in open visits, though video taping of other visits has been routine as a security precaution.

2. By Legal Advisers

04–83 Prisoners are entitled to be visited by their legal adviser at any reasonable time for the purposes of consulting in relation to any legal matter in which the prisoner is, or may be, involved (rule 58(1)). Such visits may take place within the sight, but must be outwith the hearing, of an officer (rule 58(2)).

3. By Procurators Fiscal

A procurator fiscal, or any person authorised by him may, in the course of his duties, visit and examine a prisoner at any reasonable time (rule 59(1)). Again, such visits must be held in sight but outwith the hearing of an officer (rule 59(2)).

04–84

4. Visits by Police

With the written authority of a procurator fiscal or chief constable, a police officer may visit any prisoner for the purposes of interviewing him, provided the prisoner is willing to be interviewed. He may also see any prisoner for the purposes of identifying him or charging him with any offence. All such visits must take place within sight and hearing of an officer (rule 60).

04–85

5. By Diplomatic Services and National or International Authorities or Organisations

Foreign national prisoners, refugees and stateless persons are entitled to visits at any reasonable time from diplomatic representatives or organisations whose principal purpose is to serve the interests of refugees or stateless persons or to protect the civil rights of such persons. All such visits must take place within the sight, but outwith the hearing of an officer unless the prisoner or the visitor otherwise requests (rule 61(1)(2)(4)).

04–86

6. Visits by the Scottish Council for Civil Liberties

Any prisoner can receive a visit from an authorised representative of the SCCL at any reasonable time, within sight but outwith the hearing of an officer, unless either the prisoner or the visitor otherwise requests (rule 61(3)).

04–87

7. Visits to Prisoners in Connection with Further Proceedings

Prisoners who are untried, civil prisoners, appealing against sentence, or whose sentence is being appealed by the Crown, who have been remanded following conviction but pending

04–88

sentence, or who are subject to further charges, are entitled to visits by registered medical practitioners or other people in connection with the further proceedings (rule 62(1)(1)). Such visits must take place within the sight of an officer, but only within his hearing if they are visits by non-medically qualified persons and the governor has so ordered (rule 62(4)).

8. Control of Admission of Visitors

04–89 All visitors to a prison are subject to the following regulations. Before admitting a visitor to a prison, an officer may ask the visitor to state his name, address and the purpose of his visit, and to deposit for the duration of the visit any article in his possession which the officer considers may be prejudicial to security, good order or safety (rule 86(1)). If the officer considers that the visitor is in possession of any prohibited article, he may ask the visitor to consent to a search of his person and any personal possessions, and of his open mouth by visual examination without the use of force or any instrument (rule 86(2)). Removal of visitors' clothing, apart from outer coat, headgear, gloves and jacket, is not authorised (rule 86(3)). If the visitor refuses to be searched, the officer may refuse admission to the prison (rule 86(4)). An officer also has the power to detain any person who brings or attempts to bring any unauthorised article into the prison under section 41(3) of the 1989 Act as substituted by section 153(4) of the 1994 Act. Such detention is subject to the same conditions as detentions under section 2 of the Criminal Justice (Scotland) Act 1980 (1989 Act, sections 41(4)–(9) as inserted by section 153(4) of the 1994 Act.) When a visitor does consent to a search, it must be carried out as expeditiously and decently as possible, by an officer of the same sex as the visitor and outwith the sight of any prisoner, other visitors or officers not of the same sex as the visitor (rule 86(5)). An officer may terminate a visit at any time if he has reasonable grounds for suspecting that a visitor is bringing in or taking out, or attempting to do either, anything which may be prejudicial to security, good order or safety, or if the visitor's conduct is prejudicial to good order or discipline (rule 86(6)). Any refusal of admission or termination of a visit must be recorded, along with the reason therefor (rule 86(7)). Governors must ensure that a notice explaining all provisions relating to visitors shall be prominently displayed in the visitors' area of the prison (rule 86(8)).

7. Viewing of Prisons

Only persons authorised by statute and those allowed by the governor or Secretary of State may be permitted to view a prison, and no one is permitted to take any photograph, make a sketch or communicate with any prisoner unless similarly authorised (rule 87(1)(2)). No photograph may be taken of a prisoner without the prisoner's prior consent (rule 87(3)). 04–90

8. Offences by Visitors

It is an offence for any person to bring or introduce or attempt by any means to bring or introduce into a prison any item not authorised by the Rules or directions (1989 Act, section 41(1)). Conveying such an item to a prisoner outside the prison or leaving it anywhere outside the prison with the intention that it shall come into the possession of a prisoner also constitutes this offence (section 41(2)), and the maximum penalty is a fine not exceeding level 3, or imprisonment not exceeding 30 days. If the items involved also violate a provision of the criminal law, the penalties applicable for possession under that law will apply. Prison officers have the power to apprehend any person offending against this provision (section 41(3)). 04–91

Work

Every convicted prisoner over the age of 16 may be required to work in prison (rule 68(1)), unless he is excused from work or any particular class of work by the medical officer on medical grounds, or by the governor on any other grounds, or is attending an educational class or counselling, both of which may be counted in lieu of work (rules 68(2)(3), 72(3), 73(2)). Each prisoner's programme of work, education and counselling must be established in consultation with the prisoner, with the objective of improving the prospects for the prisoner's successful reintegration into the community, his morale, attitude and self-respect (rule 67). 04–92

Except with the permission of the governor, no prisoner may work in the service of another prisoner or an officer (rule 04–93

68(4)). No prisoner can be forced to work, or attend educational classes in lieu of work, for more than 40 hours a week (excluding meal breaks), and everyone is entitled to at least one rest day per week (rule 69(1)(2)). As far as is practicable, prisoners should not be required to work on the recognised day of observance of their declared religion, or on such other days recognised by their denomination and approved by direction (rule 69(3)). Prisoners are entitled to work in association with other prisoners unless the governor has ordered that they be kept out of association (see, *supra*, *Association*).

04–94   Governors must take account of the interests and need of prisoners to obtain useful skills and experiences in providing a range of work (rule 70(1)). However, this is qualified by the requirements of practicality and the operation and maintenance of the prison (*ibid*.). Work placements outside the prison may be provided (rule 70(2)), subject to conditions specified by the Secretary of State in a direction (rule 70(3)). The current direction restricts outside work to convicted prisoners of categories C and D considered suitable by both the governor and the medical officer. Proposed work premises and conditions must also be deemed suitable and proper arrangements must be made for the transport and, if necessary, supervision of prisoners on such placements.

04–95   Prisoners are entitled to remuneration for work, or classes or counselling undertaken in lieu of work, at a rate and subject to such conditions as the Secretary of State may determine in a direction (rule 74). The current direction allows for the payment of an advance of £2.50 for all prisoners on arrival in prison; this is deducted from the prisoners' last weekly wage. Otherwise the direction allows for two wage systems, a flat rate system, which includes a performance related element, and a bonus rated system whereunder prisoners can be paid in accordance with their productivity. Prisoners undertaking education or counselling instead of work are entitled to be paid the same amount as they received in the last week in which they worked. Equally, prisoners in the prison hospital receive the minimum weekly pay appropriate to their last job, and prisoners in outside hospitals receive a flat rate of £3.50. Prisoners on home leave receive £6.00 for a three day period and £8.00 for a five day leave, if any such leave falls within the normal working week. All prisoners receive with their wages the sum equivalent to the cost of a second class postage stamp, and only this element of the wage cannot be stopped as a disciplinary punishment under rule 100. Untried and civil prisoners cannot be forced to work, but may volunteer to do so (rule 71). Those who do work, or take education or counselling as an alternative, receive the same earnings as convicted prisoners (rule 71(2)).

Provisions Relating to Other Classes of Prisoners

1. Female Prisoners

Female prisoners must be accommodated in rooms or cells which are entirely separate from those used for male prisoners (rule 114). Subject to any directions made by the Secretary of State, the governor may permit a female prisoner to have her baby with her in prison, and must provide everything necessary for the baby's maintenance (rule 116). Additional articles or food for the baby's maintenance or care may, at the discretion of the governor, be provided at the expense of the prisoner or some other person (*ibid.*).   **04–96**

The medical officer is under a duty to notify the governor of any female prisoner who is pregnant or is likely to give birth during the period of her imprisonment (rule 115(1)). The governor must not notify any friend or relative of the prisoner that she is pregnant without the consent of the prisoner unless the prisoner is incapable because of illness of giving such consent and the governor has no reason to believe that consent would be withheld (rule 115(2)). A pregnant prisoner who is kept out of association with other prisoners must be kept under supervision as far as is reasonably practicable and she may be required to share a cell or room with another suitable prisoner if the governor or medical officer consider that this is appropriate; she must not be required to do work of a strenuous nature in the later stages of pregnancy and must be supplied with food and drink which take into account any special dietary requirements (rule 115(3)). The medical officer must make arrangements for the prisoner to be transferred to an outside hospital for the purposes of giving birth to the baby (rule 115(4)).   **04–97**

The vast majority of female prisoners are kept in Cornton Vale prison, though there are facilities for holding small   **04–98** numbers in Aberdeen, Inverness and Dumfries. The overall small number of female prisoners renders it more difficult to provide the same range of facilities for different needs within the population as is available for male prisoners, but steps have recently been taken to allow appropriate female prisoners the same freedoms as males in security categories C and D.

2. Untried Prisoners

04–99   Untried prisoners are all those committed to prison for examination or trial on any criminal charge, those remanded in custody under the Extradition Act 1989 and those detained under Schedule 2 or 3 to the Immigration Act 1971, but excluding any such prisoner serving a sentence of imprisonment (rule 3(1)).

04–100   Untried prisoners must, as far as possible, be kept apart from other categories of prisoner (rule 14). They may, at their own expense, be visited by a medical or dental practitioner of their own choosing (rule 34), and be entitled to keep in their possession and smoke tobacco, to a maximum of 62.5 grammes or 50 cigarettes, and purchased from the prison canteen (rule 41). In each of these cases, only the prisoner or someone outwith the prison can provide the cash or goods mentioned. It should be noted that possession and use of tobacco are rights for this group of prisoners, while they are privileges for convicted prisoners. However, each of these rights may be withdrawn as a punishment for breach of prison discipline (rule 100(1)).

04–101   Untried prisoners cannot be forced to work or undertake educational classes under rule 71 (rule 66(1)), but, if they volunteer, they may be paid at the same rate as convicted prisoners (rule 71).

04–102   The same rules as apply in relation to visits by a person of a convicted prisoner's choice apply to untried prisoners, with the exception that they are entitled to a visit of a minimum of 30 minutes' duration each day of the week except Saturday and Sunday, or, if they have not had a visit each weekday, a 30-minute visit on Saturday or Sunday (rule 56(2)). In addition, untried prisoners are entitled to visits by registered medical practitioners, or any other person whom it is necessary for the prisoner to consult in relation to any proceedings in respect of which he is committed to or detained in prison, or complying with any condition of bail requiring the deposit of a sum of money (rule 62). Such visits must be allowed at times and for periods which the governor considers reasonable, may involve no more than three visitors at any one time, and must be conducted within sight but outwith the hearing of an officer, save when the governor orders a non-medical visit to be listened to by an officer (*ibid.*).

Untried prisoners may only be photographed on written application by a procurator fiscal or police officer of not lower rank than a superintendent, but palm and finger prints may be taken at any time (rule 10(5)). Any photographs, including negatives and copies, or palm or finger prints so taken must be immediately destroyed if the prisoner is released before trial or disposal of proceedings against him, or if he is acquitted after trial (rule 10(6)). While untried, a prisoner can only be allocated to security categories A or B (rule 12(4)).   **04–103**

Untried prisoners are subject to the same disciplinary procedures as convicted prisoners, and any award of additional days as a punishment may be made prospectively, but will take effect only if the eventual sentence is ordered to commence before the date of sentence (1989 Act, section 39(7) as added by section 24 of the 1993 Act, rule 100(2)). The maximum period for which an award by a governor may be suspended in relation to an untried prisoner is three months (rule 101(1)).   **04–104**

3. Civil Prisoners

Civil prisoners are those committed to prison for contempt of court, or failure to pay a fine imposed therefor, breach of interdict, non-compliance with an order under section 45 of the Court of Session Act 1988, or by order under sections 4 or 6 of the Civil Imprisonment (Scotland) Act 1882, or by a warrant issued under section 1(1) of the Law Reform (Miscellaneous Provisions) (Scotland) Act 1940 (rule 3(1)). Civil prisoners are treated in all regards like untried prisoners, save that the Rules require that they be kept apart from each other, and from other classes of prisoners, as far as is reasonably practicable (rule 14).   **04–105**

4. Young Offenders

Convicted persons in the age range 16 to 21 cannot be sentenced to imprisonment, but may be sentenced to   **04–106** detention (Criminal Procedure (Scotland) Act 1975, section 45, as amended). Section 19 of the 1989 Act enables the Secretary of State to provide young offenders institutions, and section 21 of the same Act authorises the continued detention of a person sentenced under the age of 21 in such an institution until the day before his 23rd birthday. Section 20A of the 1989 Act, added by section 23 of the 1993 Act, authorises the detention of persons under 21 in a prison or remand centre, but only for a temporary purpose if the person is under the age of 18.

04–107   The main difference between the rules governing young offenders' institutions and those governing prisons relates to the constitution of visiting committees. Members of committees for young offender establishments are to be appointed by the Secretary of State, and at least two of them must be justices of the peace (1989 Act, section 19(3)). The other difference between the two types of establishment is that, where adult prisoners are entitled to take exercise and spend time in the open air (rule 75), young offenders are entitled to such physical recreation, training and exercise as is required to promote health and physical well being (Schedule 1(3)).

5. Young Prisoners

04–108   Prisoners under the age of 16 (mainly children held on "unruly certificates" or sentenced to be detained in a place to be chosen by the Secretary of State) are entitled to a minimum of two half-hour visits each week (unless they are also untried prisoners) (rule 55(3)). They cannot be forced to work, but the governor must arrange a programme of education suitable to their needs (rules 66(2), 72(2)). No arrangements need be made to keep the different categories of young prisoner separate (rule 14). Young prisoners are not allowed access to tobacco in any circumstances and cannot be subject to cellular confinement as a punishment for disciplinary infractions (rule 100(1)(d)).

CHAPTER 5

DISCIPLINE AND COMPLAINTS SYSTEMS

Discipline

1. Criminal Justice Process

The writ of the ordinary criminal law continues to run within **05–01** penal establishments and any matter which could constitute a criminal offence may be reported to the police and dealt with in the normal way. The only material difference is that prisoners who are already detained on a valid warrant and are charged with further offences are not entitled to the protection of the 110 and 40 day rules. Accordingly, the start of their trials can be delayed beyond these limits, but subject to the requirement that the summons or indictment is served within the usual time-limits.

In practice, however, considerable discretion is left to **05–02** governors, staff and prisoners in relation to reporting matters to the police. If a prisoner asks for the police to be brought in to investigate any matter, the governor must allow this. Equally, if a member of staff alleges that an assault has been committed against him, he can insist that the matter is referred to the police. In any other situation, the governor has the power to decide whether to call in the police or to deal with it in the internal disciplinary system.

Several factors combine to make references to the police **05–03** relatively unattractive. First, there is inevitably some delay in the investigation of the incident and in bringing any case to trial. It is often important in the context of the prison to have such matters resolved speedily. Staff and prisoners must go on interacting with each other within the close confines of the establishment pending resolution of the issue, and the sooner this can be achieved, the better.

Secondly, it can be difficult to conduct a police **05–04** investigation in the normal way within a penal establishment. Especially difficult may be finding corroborating evidence, given that many alleged incidents take place when only the two people involved are present. Equally, there may be reluctance on the part of some possible witnesses to co-operate with an outside body, a reluctance which may be lessened when the investigation is conducted internally.

05–05   Thirdly, given that an alternative internal procedure is available, prosecuting authorities might be reluctant to take proceedings on what are seen outwith the prison as minor matters. It is not always the case that persons with no experience of the prison environment appreciate fully the impact some incidents can have in the closed environment of the prison.

05–06   Fourthly, the very organisation of court proceedings poses particular difficulties, and attracts much higher costs, when possible witnesses are serving prisoners who may require considerable security precautions when taken outwith the prison.

05–07   Finally, the range of sentences available to courts in dealing with persons already serving sentences of imprisonment is not always appropriate. Thus, for example, a prisoner serving life imprisonment can be sentenced to further periods of detention, but it does not seem very sensible to add to a life sentence and, especially near the start of such a sentence, the impact on the prisoner may be small. Equally, there may be a temptation for courts to order additional sentences to be concurrent with existing determinate sentences, with the net result that there is effectively no additional punishment. The non-custodial sentences available to courts have little meaning for serving prisoners, unless the prisoner is nearing the end of the prison sentence. Courts cannot, of course, impose sentences which restrict prisoners' access to privileges or facilities within the prison.

05–08   Accordingly, while obviously serious matters are naturally referred to the police, there may be a tendency for less serious matters to be dealt with internally, even when they may constitute criminal offences.

2. Internal Disciplinary Mechanisms

05–09   Section 39 of the 1989 Act empowers the Secretary of State to make Rules for, *inter alia*, "the discipline and control" of prisoners and adds; "Rules made under this section shall make provision for ensuring that a person who is charged with any offence under the rules shall be given a proper opportunity of presenting his case" (section 39(1)(2)). The 1952 Rules (rules 38–47) gave the governor, or, in more serious cases, the visiting committee, authority to adjudicate on alleged commission of the offences specified in rule 42, and to impose penalties ranging from deprivation of privileges to loss of remission. In conformity with section 39(2) of the Act, the Rules also specified that "Before a report is adjudicated the prisoner concerned shall be informed of the offence for which he has been reported, and shall be given an opportunity of hearing the facts alleged against him and of being heard in his own defence" (rule 40(1)).

The English equivalent of these Rules, and practices under them, both of which were virtually identical, gave rise to several challenges before English domestic courts and the European Court of Human Rights. The domestic courts had resisted attempts by prisoners to persuade them to intervene in any way with prison processes, with Lord Denning giving the famous justification, "If the courts were to entertain actions by disgruntled prisoners the governor's life would be made intolerable" (*Becker* v. *Home Office* [1972] 2 Q.B. 407). In 1984, however, this began to change.   **05–10**

The change requires to be understood in its context. The main factor, it is suggested, was the report of the European Commission in the case of *Campbell and Fell* v. *U.K.* (1982) 5 E.H.R.R. 207. In that case, two prisoners who had been brought before the board of visitors (the English equivalent of the Scottish visiting committee) had requested legal representation on the grounds that they stood to lose considerable amounts of remission and, in order properly to present their own cases, required the services of a defence lawyer. The board had refused this application and had proceeded to find the prisoners guilty and order forfeiture of remission. The prisoners sought redress under article 6 of the Convention, which provides that "In the determination of his civil rights and obligations or of any criminal charge against him, everyone is entitled to a fair and public hearing ... by an independent and impartial tribunal ... [and] to defend himself in person or through legal assistance of his own choosing". In the first part of the proceedings under the Convention, the prisoners were successful. The Commission ruled that their freedom was at issue in the adjudication, and that they were therefore entitled to the protections enshrined in article 6.   **05–11**

In the meantime, another case on the same issue had commenced in the domestic courts. A Mr Tarrant and another prisoner appeared before a board of visitors and applied for permission to be legally represented. This was   **05–12** refused, but the adjudication was adjourned to allow the prisoners to challenge the decision. The case came to court in 1984 and it was held that, in view of the seriousness of the penalties available to the board of visitors, the board should at least have considered whether legal representation should be allowed to the prisoner (*R. v. Secretary of State for the Home Department and others, ex p. Tarrant and Another* [1985] Q.B. 251). Board of visitor and visiting committee adjudications were immediately suspended while the respective departments considered the position. The European Court of Human Rights then produced its judgment in the *Campbell and Fell* case (1984) 7 E.H.R.R. 165, confirming part of the Commission's conclusion, but stressing that the crucial factor for it was the amount of remission which the prisoners stood to lose before the board of visitors. (In "very serious cases" in England, and in all cases referred to them in Scotland, the board of visitors and the visiting committees had unrestricted powers to award remission loss as a punishment.)

05–13   Both the Home Office and the Scottish Office then produced proposals for making legal representation available before the respective adjudicators, with provision for the legal aid system to meet the cost. Legal representation was to be available at the discretion of the adjudicating body rather than as of right. In Scotland it was never granted, but this was the result of a policy change which effectively prevented any further cases being referred to the visiting committees. The 1994 Scottish Rules now make no provision for the visiting committees to have any jurisdiction in these matters. The system south of the border continued, with regular grants of legal representation, until the power of the boards to hold adjudications was finally abolished in 1991.

05–14   In both the *Tarrant* and *Campbell and Fell* cases, reference had been made to governors' adjudications as well. Given that the power of governors to award loss of remission was limited, in Scotland to 14 days and in England and Wales to 28 days, it is probably the case that the European Court of Human Rights would not, on the ratio of its decision in *Campbell and Fell*, have held that article 6 applied. The court in *Tarrant* left the matter open. Not surprisingly, there quickly followed attempts to have governors' adjudications subjected to review by the courts.

05–15   In the first of these cases, *R. v. Deputy Governor of Camp Hill Prison, ex p. King* [1985] Q.B. 735, it was held that governors' adjudications were not subject to judicial review;

shortly afterwards, a Northern Irish court came to the opposite conclusion (*R. v. Governor of H.M. Prison, The Maze, ex p. McKiernan* (1985) 6 N.I.J.B. 6). The matter was finally resolved in *Leech* v. *Deputy Governor, Parkhurst Prison* [1988] A.C. 533, the court held that judicial review was competent since governors are exercising powers under statute which affect the "rights or legitimate expectations" of subjects, and must therefore act in accordance with the rules of natural justice. The Scottish courts have followed this line in *Doran* v. *Secretary of State*, 1990 G.W.D. 26–1431.

New instructions have been issued to governors south of the border to ensure compliance with the normal requirements of natural justice. Change in Scotland has been much slower. Accordingly, many of the old practices surrounding adjudications continued until the promulgation of the 1994 Rules. Prisoners were generally given only verbal notice of the charges they had to face, were often confined to their cells between the time of the alleged incident and the holding of the adjudication, were not seated, had no note taking facilities during the hearing, and could not question witnesses directly or insist on witnesses being called on their own behalf. In addition, charges were often lacking in specificity, with much use being made of multiple charges arising from the one incident, and considerable use made of general charges like "committing a nuisance" and "In any way offending against good order and discipline". Finally, there was no set standard of proof for hearings, and no right of appeal against any finding or punishment (though the prisoner could petition the Secretary of State, who had authority to change the punishment but not to set aside the finding of guilt). There has been discussion for some time about the issue of new guidelines to governors about the holding of adjudications. It is understood that there have also been some pilot projects where prisoners have been issued with written charge sheets and allowed to be seated during the hearing. But in many establishments, the old practices continued up to the issue of the new Rules. Accordingly, there may still be prisoners in the system who are subject to punishments awarded under the old system. **05–16**

3. Current Position

The 1994 Rules go a considerable way to remedying the situation. They not only redraft the list of offences and **05–17** amend the punishments which can be awarded, but they also specify in greater detail the procedures to be followed, and establish for the first time an explicit standard of proof, and an appeal mechanism against both findings of guilt and punishments imposed.

(a) Breaches of Discipline

05–18   Schedule 3 to the Rules provides as follows:

A prisoner shall be guilty of a breach of discipline if he:

(*a*) commits any assault;

(*b*) detains any person against his will;

(*c*) denies access to any part of the prison to any officer;

(*d*) fights with any person;

(*e*) intentionally endangers the health or personal safety of others, or, by his conduct, is reckless, whereby such health or personal safety is endangered;

(*f*) intentionally obstructs an officer in the execution of his duty;

(*g*) escapes or absconds from prison or from legal custody;

(*h*) fails—

  (i) to return when he should return after being temporarily released under Part 4 of these Rules; or

  (ii) to comply with any condition upon which he is so temporarily released;

(*i*) has in his possession—

  (i) any article which he is not authorised to have; or

  (ii) a greater quantity of any article than he is authorised to have; or

  (iii) any article in a part of a prison in which he is not authorised to have it;

(*j*) sells or delivers to any person any article which he is not authorised to have;

(*k*) sells or, without permission, delivers to any person any article which he is allowed to have only for his own use;

(*l*) takes improperly any article belonging to another person or to the prison;

(m) intentionally or recklessly sets fire to any part of a prison or any other property, whether or not that property belongs to him;

(n) destroys or damages any part of a prison or any other property, other than his own;

(o) absents himself from any place where he is required to be or is present at any place where he is not authorised to be;

(p) is disrespectful to any officer or any person visiting a prison;

(q) uses threatening, abusive or insulting words or behaviour;

(r) intentionally fails to work properly or, being required to work, refuses to do so;

(s) disobeys any lawful order;

(t) disobeys or fails to comply with any rule or regulation applying to a prisoner;

(u) inhales any substance, or the fumes of any substance, which is a prohibited article or consumes, takes, injects or ingests any substance which is a prohibited article;

(v) commits any indecent or obscene act; or

(w) attempts to commit, incites another prisoner to commit, or assists another prisoner to commit, any of the foregoing breaches.

The list is manifestly comprehensive. It provides better **05–19** specificity than the previous list and there should accordingly be less need to resort to general charges. There may be some concern over offences like "fights with any person", in that the formulation seems to differentiate this from "assault" and might therefore exclude a defence of self-defence. It remains to be seen how this is operated in practice.

(b) Punishments Available to Governors

Rule 100 provides for the continuation of many of the **05–20** original punishments, but adds the possibility of a caution, restricts the award of loss of privileges to those privileges granted under rule 40 (see Chapter 4), and restricts the imposition of forfeiture of a prisoner's right to wear his own clothes to cases involving escapes or attempts to escape. Thus the major punishments available to the governor are: a caution, forfeiture of privileges for a period not exceeding 14 days, stoppage of wages for a period not exceeding 56 days, to a maximum of 28 days earnings, cellular confinement not exceeding three days, forfeiture of remission for those sentenced before October 1, 1993 for a period not exceeding 14 days, additional days for those sentenced on or after October 1, 1993 to a maximum of 14 days for any one offence and a cumulative maximum of one sixth of the total sentence, and forfeiture of the right to wear one's own clothing for such a period as may be specified (rule 100). Governors are also entitled to suspend any punishment imposed (other than a caution), for a maximum period of six months (three months for remand prisoners) (rule 101). On commission of a further offence against discipline during any period of suspension, the governor dealing with the new offence may direct that the suspended punishment should take effect in full or in part, vary the period of suspension up to the maximum of six months from the date of variation, or give no direction with respect to the suspended punishment (*ibid.*).

05–21 Punishments of additional days, but not loss of remission, have the effect of postponing a prisoners eligibility for parole consideration as well as his right to release at two-thirds sentence (1989 Act, section 39(7)), as inserted by 1993 Act, section 24). The same section allows governors to award additional days conditionally upon a remand prisoner being sentenced to imprisonment on the charges for which he is currently being held (section 39(7)(b)), but under the 1994 Rules, this only applies if the prisoner's subsequent sentence is backdated from the date of sentence (Rule 100(2)(b)).

(c) Procedure

05–22 Every suspected breach of discipline must be reported forthwith in writing to the governor by the officer to whose notice it has come, and the governor may order the prisoner to be kept apart from other prisoners until the adjudication (rule 95(2)). It should be noted that the power to order the separation of the prisoner from others is a discretionary one. It should thus not be exercised routinely. The maximum period for which the governor can authorise removal from association is 72 hours, though the Secretary of State may authorise further periods of one month at a time (rule 95(3)(4)). As soon as the adjudication has been held, any such authorisation lapses (*ibid.*).

05–23 Charges must be brought as soon as possible and, save in exceptional circumstances, within 48 hours of discovery of the alleged offence (rule 96(1)). The prisoner must be served with a written notice of the charge at least two hours before the hearing (rule 96(2)). Save in exceptional circumstances, the hearing must be held no later than the day after the charge is laid, unless that day is a Sunday or public holiday (rule 97(1)). Before the hearing starts, the governor must satisfy himself that the prisoner has had sufficient time to prepare his case and must adjourn the case, if he considers this is reasonable, to allow the prisoner further time to prepare, or if there are other reasonable grounds for doing so (rule 97(2)(3)). The prisoner must be given a full opportunity of hearing what is alleged against him, presenting his own case and calling witnesses on his own behalf (rule 97(4)). The governor may refuse to allow the prisoner to call any witness, but only if the governor is satisfied, after discussing the matter with the prisoner, that the evidence the witness would give is of no relevance or value in the case (rule 97(5)). Prisoners may elect to sit or stand during the hearing (rule 97(6)). When the governor considers, in exceptional circumstances, that legal representation for the prisoner is necessary, the governor may permit this on the application of the prisoner (rule 97(7)).

There are no restrictions on the kind of evidence, or the **05–24** form of it, which a governor may take into account in deciding a case, but the evidence of a person who has not given oral evidence at the inquiry may only be taken into account with the consent of the prisoner (rule 98(1)(2)). The standard of proof is whether the charge has been proved beyond reasonable doubt (rule 98(3)). Accordingly, the normal criminal standard of proof must be applied. Before imposing any punishment after a finding of guilt, the governor must afford the prisoner an opportunity of making a plea in mitigation (rule 98(4)).

Breaches of discipline occurring immediately before a **05–25** prisoner is transferred to another establishment may be adjudicated upon at the establishment to which the prisoner is transferred (rule 99).

(d) Appeals

Prisoners have the right to appeal against a finding of **05–26** guilt and the punishment imposed, or against the punishment only (rule 111(1)). When the case was heard by someone other than the governor of the prison, the appeal is to the internal complaints committee (see below); where the governor heard the original case, the appeal is to the Secretary of State (rule 111(2)). The governor has the power to quash a finding of guilt and remit or mitigate any punishment not already served; the Secretary of State may order a governor to quash a finding of guilt or remit, mitigate or substitute another punishment (rule 111(4)). It is thought likely that the Independent Complaints Commissioner will have a function in relation to appeals against findings and sentences of disciplinary hearings.

05–27   Governors also have the power to restore forfeited remission or rescind awards of additional days on the written application of the prisoner (rule 112(1)). In deciding such applications the governor must take into account the prisoner's subsequent behaviour, and must inform the prisoner of his decision within seven days of the date on which the application was made (rule 112(2)(3)).

(e) Comment

05–28   During the parliamentary stages of the 1993 Act, an undertaking was made that procedures for governors' orderly rooms would be subject to new instructions from the Secretary of State (*Hansard* H.L. Vol. 538, cols. 556–558). It is to be hoped that these new procedures will come into force quickly so that prisoners' faith in the process may be improved. The powers available to governors are significant, amounting in effect to the power to impose an additional sentence of imprisonment, or to make an important difference to how the prisoner experiences daily life in the prison. It is accordingly necessary that the procedures are fair, and are seen to be fair, to all parties. The vast majority of prisoners will no doubt continue to accept their guilt of disciplinary infractions and the punishments imposed on them; but it is crucial that the procedure is able to cope properly with contested cases.

05–29   The explicit authorisation in the rules of legal representation at hearings is a sign that the significance of the hearings is being recognised. It was difficult to understand the rationale of the European Court of Human Rights in using the *amount* of remission at risk as the criterion for deciding whether article 6, which talks only of freedom and civil rights, should apply. Perhaps the new terminology of "additional days" makes much clearer the point that governors are effectively imposing additional prison sentences in these instances, and thus article 6 clearly would apply. If the new system recognises this without the need to be forced into change by external court decisions it will be a sign of the SPS's commitment to the rule of law.

Complaints

The importance of a proper complaints system within the **05–30** relatively closed world of the prison is best summed up in a quotation from the Prior Report:

> Control in prisons derives from three main elements: the quality of the relationship between staff and prisoners, the provision of a wide range of purposeful activities for prisoners and procedures that are demonstrably fair for enforcing rules and responding to complaints (*Report of the Committee on the Prison Disciplinary System*, Cmnd. 9641 (1985), paragraph 2.19).

Prisons are, by their nature, closed institutions. Prisoners **05–31** are, generally, kept against their will. They rely for almost every requirement of daily life on the prison staff. The staff can control access both to anything outside the prison and to everything inside it. The potential for abuse of this power is great; so, too, may be the tendency for the unwilling residents to complain about every aspect of their situation, including matters beyond the power of the prison staff. Securing good order and discipline with proper regard for the rule of law thus requires an efficient and effective system of controls, only part of which can be provided by a good complaints system.

The first priority, therefore, must be to ensure that justified **05–32** complaints are as few as possible. Good staff recruitment and training policies are the best initial contribution to achieving this aim. Staff training has been accorded a high priority in recent years, with training officer posts having been established at each institution in addition to greatly increased resources at the SPS staff college. Proper supervision and accountability systems are the next requirement, especially as more power is devolved to individual institutions and to staff of basic grades. But no matter how good the recruitment and training programmes are, and no matter how efficient the management supervision may be, there will also always be the need for a formal complaints system in penal establishments, to enable issues which are missed by these systems to be addressed, and to enable those systems themselves to be brought to account.

05–33   *Custody and Care* gave an undertaking that a review of the complaints system in Scottish prisons would be undertaken, and the SPS in due course produced a discussion paper on the issue, *Right and Just* (1993). The system proposed in this document would have involved, in addition to officers and governors, the establishment of two levels of independent grievance panel, a local one for each establishment and a national one, which would have had original jurisdiction in relation to certain matters, and an appellate one in relation to matters referred to the local panels. It would appear, however, that these proposals did not meet with much favour in the consultation process. Instead, the SPS introduced a new internal complaints and requests system in February 1994, to be headed by an independent Prisons Complaints Commissioner. This system is described below and is in addition to the external mechanisms which will continue to be available to prisoners.

(a) Complaints/Requests Mechanisms within the SPS

05–34   The management philosophy of the SPS is that all decisions should be taken at the lowest appropriate level within the hierarchical structure of the service. Consistently with this, rule 3, the interpretation section of the new Rules, defines "governor" in such a way that the governor in charge of the establishment is not obliged personally to exercise all of the powers granted him by the Rules. The governor in charge no longer has the duty previously imposed on him (1952 Rules, rule 50) to see prisoners himself. However, the new system provides for the governor in charge to be available to prisoners within the hierarchy of avenues, and for prisoners to raise sensitive or serious issues at the level of governor in charge without going through the earlier stages (rules 107, 108).

05–35   The new internal system is as follows:

Requests/Complaints in Scottish Prisons

Prisons Complaints Commissioner

This office was established in Autumn 1994 and the appointee is responsible for establishing a system for responding, within time-scales to be established, to prisoners' complaints. The office has jurisdiction over all matters for which the SPS is responsible, including adjudications, but will not be competent to deal with any matter concerning sentencing or parole. It is envisaged that the majority of cases will be dealt with on a paper only basis, with the commissioner having a right of access to all prison books and papers. The commissioner will be independent of the SPS, and will make recommendations to the Chief Executive of the SPS. An annual report will be submitted to the Secretary of State.

Secretary of State for Scotland

De novo matters concerning transfers and allegations against the governor in charge of a prison may be raised by a prisoner directly at this level. Otherwise all applications must have come through the stages below. Applications must be in writing and should normally be replied to, in writing and with reasons for decisions, within 14 days (rule 109).

Governor In Charge

Prisoners may raise sensitive or serious matters directly at this stage under a confidential access procedure involving sealed application to the governor (rule 108). Otherwise all matters must have been raised at earlier stages of the process. All applications must be in writing and the governor may deal with them on paper or by having a meeting with the applicant. Answers, with reasons, must normally be provided in writing within seven days (rule 107).

Internal Complaints Committee

Each establishment must appoint a complaints committee consisting of at least three members of staff, one of whom must be a governor residential. Prisoners cannot be members of this committee. Appeals to the committee must be in writing and reasoned replies, in writing, must be given by the committee, usually within seven days. The committee will hold a hearing at which the prisoner may be present, call witnesses (subject to the chairman's discretion) and be represented. The committee's function is to advise the governor in charge, and it is expected that the governor will accept any recommendations made by the committee (rule 106).

Residential Unit Manager

As the first line of appeal, complaints to residential unit managers against decisions of gallery officers must be in writing and should usually be answered, with reasons and in writing, within 24 hours (rule 105).

Residential Officer

It is hoped that the vast majority of complaints and applications can be resolved informally at this level. There is no requirement for applications to be in writing, but if they are, they must normally be responded to, in writing and with reasons, within one day (rule 104).

05–36   With the exception of those matters noted in the text, all applications must go through each stage of the process in order if the prisoner wishes to continue raising the complaint. Standard application forms are available to prisoners, and copies of replies are made available to applicants and kept on the applicant's prison file.

(b) Other Mechanisms Peculiar to Prisons

(i) Visiting sheriffs and justices of the peace

05–37   The powers of visiting sheriffs and justices of the peace are restricted to noting their observations in a book to be kept for that purpose by the governor, who must bring any such minute to the attention of the visiting committee at its next visit (1989 Act, section 15). It is thought that in practice prisoners do not avail themselves of this avenue for raising complaints.

(ii) Visiting committees

05–38   The powers of the visiting committee were discussed in Chapter 3, where it was seen that they have no executive authority but can only report their opinion to the Secretary of State. Research evidence indicates that prisoners have little faith in the visiting committees in this role. Not only did many prisoners not know that the committees can perform this function, but those who were aware of this power did not see the committees as genuinely independent of the governor or as able to challenge the governor's decisions (McManus and Tuck, *Visiting Committees in Scottish Penal Establishments* (1985) SHHD). Since publication of that report, there has been some improvement in the performance of some visiting committees. Local and national training for committee members has improved. Some committees have adopted a stricter rota for attendance at their prisons and have developed mechanisms for allowing prisoners direct access to the committee without having to inform prison staff. The new appointment system and requirements for attendance in the 1994 Rules may serve to improve the situation further. Committees have an obvious potential in this role. They can see the prisoner quickly and allow him the opportunity for a personal hearing; their investigation of any matter can be speedily carried out in the prison, using their right of access to all places and books, and they can communicate the outcome directly to the prisoner. But it probably remains the case that factors like their historical inactivity in this area, the members' comparative lack of knowledge of the details of prison life, their resultant reliance on prison staff, and the limited power available to the committees, will continue to render them less than attractive to most prisoners as a method of resolving grievances.

(iii) Her Majesty's Chief Inspector of Prisons (HMCIP)

HMCIP has no role in dealing with individual prisoner's complaints. He may, of course, be concerned with how the procedures for dealing with complaints are being operated within individual prisons, and may also concern himself with matters which appear to be the subject of complaints from a number of prisoners. It is now part of the normal working practices of the inspectorate to interview groups of prisoners during the regular inspections of each establishment, and to record the main points arising from these discussions in the reports submitted to the Secretary of State.

05–39

(c) External Mechanisms

Prisoners retain the ordinary rights of the subject to seek redress of any grievance through petitions to Parliament and the Crown. They also have access to the Parliamentary Commissioner for Administration (the Ombudsman)

05–40

through a member of parliament, in the same way as anyone else.

05–41   Access to courts is also freely available. Prisoners' correspondence to and from courts may not be read by an officer of the prison in any circumstances and may only be opened by an officer where he has cause to believe that it contains a prohibited article, and when the prisoner is present (rule 49). The same rule defines "court" to include the European Court of Justice, the European Court of Human Rights and the European Commission of Human Rights. Letters to and from legal advisers do not enjoy the same level of protection (see above).

05–42   Access to the domestic courts is totally unimpeded. Prisoners may bring legal actions about any matter at all under the same rules applying to anyone else. Actions in relation to decisions made under the Prison Act or rules may be particularly susceptible to judicial review procedure, which is geared to ensuring that public bodies discharge their functions in accordance with the rules of natural justice and the powers accorded to them by the law. For a good, brief description of the procedure adopted in such actions see Bradley, "Administrative Law", in *The Laws of Scotland* (Stair Memorial Encyclopaedia), Volume 1, paragraph 346).

05–43   Prisoners wishing to appear personally in court in relation to any civil law matter in which they are involved have no right to insist that they be produced by the prison. They may, however, apply to the Secretary of State to exercise his discretion to allow them to attend and the Secretary of State may grant permission on condition that the prisoner pay any expenses incurred. There is no decided case on this matter in Scotland, but it is suggested that the decisions in the English case of *R. v. Secretary of State for the Home Department, ex parte Wynne* [1992] Q.B. 406; would be followed in Scotland.

(d) Access to the European Commission of Human Rights

05–44   The procedure for applying to the European Commission of Human Rights is comprehensively described in a booklet published by the Council of Europe (*Making an Application to the European Commission of Human Rights*, (1987)). By circular instruction in England and Wales, copies of this booklet should be available in all prison libraries. There seems to be no equivalent provision in Scotland.

05–45   Briefly, the procedure is as follows. Before an application can be considered, the applicant must have exhausted all possible domestic remedies. In the prison context, this does not require that every single step of the complaints mechanism must be used, but if a significant step has been omitted, the Commission will declare the application inadmissible. In particular, the Commission at least does not consider that the visiting committees and the Parliamentary Commissioner for Administration are effective remedies, since neither has the power to issue binding decisions granting redress to an aggrieved person (*Boyle and Rice* v. *U.K.* (1988) 10 E.H.R.R. 425 at page 458). The application must be lodged within six months of the final decision in domestic proceedings in the case, and must relate to a matter within the remit of the Convention which has not previously been determined by the Commission or a similar international body.

If an application passes these hurdles (and the majority of applications do not), it is examined by the Commission. It will establish the facts of the case and attempt to negotiate a "friendly settlement" between the applicant and the member state. If such a settlement is reached, the Commission publishes a report and the case ends at that stage. If no settlement can be reached, the Commission draws up a report stating its opinion for submission to the Committee of Ministers. It is for this Committee to decide whether there has been a breach of the Convention. **05–46**

Either the member state involved or the Commission can, within three months of the Commission's report being sent to the Committee, refer the matter to the court. If this is done, the court may take written and oral evidence from the parties and consider this along with the Commission's report before reaching a final judgment on the matter. Decisions of the court are binding as interpretations of the Convention, but cannot be directly enforced within the U.K. by the individual concerned. The judgments in prison cases arising from the U.K. have, however, all been accepted by the U.K. government. If the case is not referred to the court, the decision of the Committee of Ministers is final. It may decide to publish the Commission's report, and can make a binding judgment. **05–47**

The procedure involved in applying to the Commission can take several years to produce a final decision, and the result is not legally enforceable within the U.K. Nonetheless, the U.K. government cannot lightly ignore adverse rulings from Strasbourg. Given that the jurisprudence of the **05–48**

Convention is continuing to develop and, in doing so, reflects the developing practices of the member states whose nationals make up the various bodies with the power to make judgments, it is not unlikely that the Convention will continue to be a source of promoting change in Scottish practices until our domestic arrangements ensure that Scottish prisons accord prisoners at least the same rights as our fellow signatories of the Convention.

Future Developments

(a) Specially for Prisoners

05–49 It may be that the rejection of the proposals in *Right and Just* was the result of changes introduced in England and Wales after publication of the Woolf report into the riot at Strangeways prison in Manchester (*Prison Disturbances April 1990*, Cm. 1456 (1991)). Woolf recommended that, in order to ensure a genuinely independent, and therefore credible, complaints system, there was a need for a complaints adjudicator for prisons (*ibid.*, paragraph 1.209(ii)). Scotland has followed this recommendation.

05–50 It remains to be seen, of course, what the result of the creation of this post and the introduction of the whole new complaints system will be. It is clearly a more formal, open and accountable system than its predecessor and complies more obviously with the requirements of natural justice. It is to be hoped that it can meet the tight time targets which it has set for itself and produce substantive as well as procedural improvements.

(b) More Generally

05–51 The ready availability of judicial review has already made challenges by prisoners through the domestic courts more common than they previously were. The 1994 Prison Rules, by incorporating many matters previously covered only by the secret standing orders and expressing many of them as entitlements, might increase this tendency. Though it is likely that the courts will not wish to involve themselves in the merits of decisions, the fact that the procedures under which decisions are reached will be more open to challenge should serve to improve decision-making processes, to the mutual benefit of prison staff and prisoners.

Further developments under the aegis of the Council of **05–52** Europe are discussed in Chapter 7. In the meantime, it is worth re-emphasising that the SPS itself has become an important catalyst for improving the legal position of prisoners and opening its actions to accountability in a variety of spheres. That very openness seems likely to lead to considerable changes in penal practices, without the intervention of outside agencies.

CHAPTER 6

RELEASE FROM CUSTODY

Temporary Release

06–01 Section 39(6) of the 1989 Act authorises the making of rules providing for the temporary release of prisoners, and rules 120–126, which are discussed fully above (Chapter 4), regulate the matter. In addition, all prisoners may be granted escorted leave for other purposes. The sentence continues to run during all such leave, as long as the permission has not been revoked and is not exceeded.

Release at End of Sentence or on Licence

A. Determinate Sentences

06–02 From the introduction of the Prisoners and Criminal Proceedings (Scotland) Act 1993 on October 1, 1993, there have been two different systems for the calculation of release dates in relation to determinate sentences of imprisonment or detention in Scotland. In general this Act was not retroactive. Accordingly, with the exceptions outlined below, persons sentenced to custody before October 1, 1993 continue to have their release dates calculated under the terms of the Prisons (Scotland) Act 1989 and the associated Prisons (Scotland) or Young Offenders (Scotland) Rules. The release of anyone sentenced on or after October 1, 1993 is governed by the 1993 Act.

06–03 Where any person's due date of release falls on a Saturday, Sunday or public holiday the release is brought forward to the immediately preceding week-day which is not a public holiday (1989 Act, section 16(1), as amended by section 27(7) of the 1993 Act).

1. Persons Sentenced before October 1, 1993

(a) Remission

06–04 Section 24 of the 1989 Act authorised the making of rules for the granting of remission to prisoners. Rule 37 of the Prison

112

(Scotland) Rules 1952, as amended, and the equivalent Young Offender rule (rule 35) established that the maximum remission which could be granted was one-third of the total sentence, with a minimum period of five days to be spent in custody. These rules applied only to convicted persons sentenced to determinate periods in custody, including those sentenced to prison or detention in default of payment of a fine. They did not apply to children sentenced under sections 206 and 413 of the 1975 Act (persons under the age of 16, or 18 if subject to a childrens hearing supervision order, sentenced to be detained in a place to be decided by the Secretary of State), nor to civil prisoners. The 1993 Act does, however, apply retrospectively to all sections 206 and 413 cases, and the release dates for these groups will be calculated in accordance with the provisions described below. The previous dispensation, which allows the Secretary of State to release these children at any time in their sentence, subject to a positive recommendation from the parole board in the cases of section 206 sentences of more than 18 months, will continue to apply, with an additional power for a local authority to order the release of a child sentenced under summary procedure to be released at any stage of the sentence (1993 Act, sections 7, 8). All other determinate sentences are calculated to the two-thirds date and the person is released on that date unless any remission has been forfeited for breach of discipline while in custody (see Chapter 5).

As a transitional measure on the introduction of the 1993   **06–05** Act, all persons in custody on October 1, 1993 serving sentences of less than two years were released on completion of one half of their sentence, subject to any loss of remission they may have incurred (Schedule 6, paragraph 3).

Post-release supervision
On release at the two-thirds stage under these provisions,   **06–06** adult prisoners are under no further liability in relation to the sentence served. They do, however, have the right to seek social work assistance in terms of section 27(1)(c) of the Social Work (Scotland) Act 1968 as inserted by section 61(4)(a) of the Law Reform (Miscellaneous Provisions) (Scotland) Act 1990, for a period of one year after release.

Young offenders sentenced to detention for a period of   **06–07** more than six months, in terms of sections 207 or 421 of the 1975 Act, are subject to compulsory social work supervision on release. Those released on parole (see below) are subject to a licence for 12 months from the date of release or until the end of the parole period, whichever is the later. Those not released on parole are subject to a licence for 12 months from the date of release, if their sentence was 18 months or more, and for six months from the date of release, if their sentence was less than 18 months. Any such licence terminates on the offender's 23rd birthday if this occurs sooner than the end of the normal licence period (1989 Act, section 32(2), (4)). During the period of the licence, released persons must comply with the conditions of the licence, which usually include regular reporting to a social worker in addition to being of good behaviour. They can be recalled to custody for a maximum period of three months for failure to comply with the licence. Recall can be authorised by the parole board or, in an emergency, by the Secretary of State, who must then refer the case to the board if the person makes representations against the recall. The board may order immediate re-release of the person. The Secretary of State retains the right to order re-release at any time during the recall period, though the person can be recalled again to serve the balance of the three month period if there is a subsequent breach of licence within the original supervision period.

06–08 Children sentenced under section 206 of the 1975 Act did not qualify for automatic remission before the 1993 Act came into effect. Those who had served half or more of a sentence less than four years, or two-thirds or more of a sentence of four years or more, on October 1, 1993 were released on that date. They are subject to a licence for a minimum of 12 months and until the expiry of the total sentence. Those who had not served one half, or two-thirds, as the case may be, of the sentence will be released when they have served the relevant portion and will be subject to a licence until a date to be determined by the parole board, such date not to be later than the date of the expiry of the total sentence (1993 Act, Schedule 6, paragraph 8). Section 413 cases will have their licence conditions and duration determined by the local authority until the expiry date of the total sentence (Schedule 6, paragraph 5).

(b) Parole

(i) Eligibility

Persons sentenced before October 1993 will continue to have **06–09** their parole eligibility governed by the 1989 Act, and any reference to a section herein is a reference to a section of that Act unless otherwise stated. Accordingly, they will be required to serve one-third of their sentence, or one year, whichever is the longer, before becoming eligible for consideration for parole (section 22(1)). Accordingly, in effect only those sentenced to more than 18 months qualify for consideration for release on parole. Parole, if granted, is subject to a licence which continues in force, unless revoked, until the two-thirds date of the sentence (section 22(8)).

(ii) Procedure **06–10**

Parole procedures will continue as before, at least for some time. Thus all cases will continue to be reviewed by a local review committee (LRC), constituted in terms of Schedule 1 paragraph 6 of the 1989 Act, until the number of cases to be considered can all be dealt with by the board itself. A dossier of reports, not prescribed in any statutory form, is compiled. This includes reports from prison staff, social workers within the prison and the community where the prisoner is proposing to live if released, the prisoner's own representations for his release and any other relevant reports from psychologists, psychiatrists or other counsellors the prisoner has seen, or from prospective employers. Reports from the police are not added unless and until the case is referred to the parole board. Prisoners are interviewed by a member of the LRC, who submits a written report to the full committee which, in turn, makes a recommendation to the Secretary of State on each case considered. Cases recommended by the local review committees are automatically sent on to the parole board; those not recommended by the LRC are subject to further vetting by officials of the Secretary of State. The cases of adult males are "prediction scored"—assessed in accordance with criteria designed to predict the likelihood of re-offending drawn up by researchers at the University of Edinburgh. If the case passes this test, it is referred to the board for consideration of release. Cases other than those of adult males are assessed by two civil servants, who may decide to refer a case to the board if they consider that, notwithstanding the recommendation of the LRC, there may be a good case for the granting of parole.

06–11   The board considers cases in full session twice a month. It has the full dossier as seen by the LRC, including the report of the LRC interviewing member and the minute of the LRC's decision in all cases, and a police report and a Crown note of circumstances of the offence in many cases. The board may decide to recommend parole, on the qualifying date or at a future date, or not to recommend parole, in which event the case will be reviewed on each annual anniversary of the qualifying date as long as there would then be a minimum of four months' parole available, or earlier if the board so recommends.

06–12   Under the 1989 Act and its predecessor, the Criminal Justice Act 1967, the board's functions are advisory only. The Secretary of State cannot release on parole without the board's positive recommendations, but he is not bound by positive recommendations. Indeed, as the courts held in *Findlay* v. *Secretary of State for the Home Department* [1985] A.C. 318, an English case under identical legislation, the Secretary of State is entitled to adopt a policy restricting the grant of parole so long as that policy allows consideration to be given to each individual case. From 1984 until 1993 in Scotland, the Secretary of State had a policy restricting the grant of parole in certain cases (*Hansard* (1984) H.C. Vol. 70, col. 90). Thus parole was normally only granted for more than a few months at the end of sentences of over five years imposed for offences involving violence, drugs or sex in "exceptional circumstances". What constituted "exceptional circumstances" was never defined, but it is known that the Secretary of State agreed with board submissions on the matter on several occasions each year.

06–13   Prisoners have no right to be given reasons for the decisions of the parole board except on return to prison after a recall (section 28(3)). The practice has been for the minute of the parole board's recommendation to be sent to the prison and for staff to be urged to use the minute in counselling the prisoner. There is, equally, no appeal against decisions of the board, though, again on recall, a prisoner is entitled to make representations in writing to the board against the decision (section 28(4)).

(iii) Parole licence conditions

Parole licences contain standard conditions, requiring the **06–14** parolee to be under the supervision of a nominated local authority, to reside in a certain area and to be of good behaviour and keep the peace. In addition, the Secretary of State may impose extra conditions in the licence, *e.g.* on alcohol or drug counselling, psychiatric treatment or residence in or away from a certain place. Breach of any of these conditions may lead to the licence being varied or revoked. Before inserting or varying any condition, the Secretary of State is obliged to consult the parole board (section 22(7)).

Revocation of a licence can be ordered by the Secretary of **06–15** State or by the board at any time until the expiry of the licence (section 28). Revocation leads to immediate recall to custody. When revocation is ordered by the Secretary of State, the case must be referred to the parole board, which may order the immediate re-release of the person. Recalled persons have the right to be told the reasons for the recall and to make written representations against it (section 28(3)). Traditionally they have had no right of access to any of the reports or materials on which the board based its decision to order the recall.

On a board recall, the board must consider any **06–16** representations subsequently made by the parolee, and can decide to order the immediate re-release of such a person. The Secretary of State must comply with such an order from the board (section 25(5)). The High Court or a sheriff court also has the power to revoke licences on conviction of a parolee of an offence punishable on indictment by imprisonment (section 28(6)), but this power has rarely been used and is not contained in the 1993 Act. Recalls can last until the prisoner reaches the normal release date of the sentence (*i.e.* with remission), but the person will be considered for re-release on parole if a further review would have been due had he not been released. If the recall is ordered by a court, the person must serve one-third of the period the licence would have remained in force or one year, whichever is the longer, before being reconsidered for release on parole (section 28(8)), though he cannot be kept beyond the date of sentence expiry.

Matters to be taken into consideration by the board in **06–17** ordering recalls have never been clearly established in case law in Scotland. The closest the courts have come to determining the matter arose in a case where a provisional release date for a life sentence prisoner was withdrawn because of adverse reports before the prisoner was actually released. In that case (*Howden* v. *Parole Board for Scotland*, 1992 G.W.D. 20–1186). the court decided that even though the prisoner had been acquitted of serious charges against him arising out of an alleged incident while on pre-parole home leave, the board was entitled to take into account information in relation to the events that had led to the charges when reviewing its earlier recommendation to the Secretary of State that the prisoner be released. The court held that the board was under an obligation to act reasonably, but that this obligation did not preclude the taking into account of any relevant information. In the case of *Rea* v. *Parole Board for Scotland*, 1993 S.L.T. 1074, a prisoner who had been granted a parole date had had it withdrawn after being involved in disciplinary proceedings within the prison. It was claimed on his behalf that he had a legitimate expectation of release on the notified date and that that date should not have been withdrawn without a hearing and the provision of full reasons. The court held that the board was entitled to take into account all information up to the date of actual release and that no particular procedural requirements had to be followed in the process. Accordingly, it seems that the board has a wide discretion as to what it considers relevant matters to be taken into account and, providing that it acts fairly, no restrictions on how it makes its decision.

2. Persons Sentenced on or after October 1, 1993

06–18 All persons sentenced to determinate sentences of imprisonment or custody on or after October 1, 1993 will have their release dates determined by the 1993 Act. The Act introduces a distinction between short-term and long-term prisoners, with the dividing line set at the moment at under four years and four years or over respectively (section 27). Subsection (2)(a) of that section allows the Secretary of State to vary these definitions by order.

(a) Short-term prisoners

06–19 Every person sentenced to less than four years, including cumulative sentences totalling less than four years (section 27(5) of the Act), now qualifies for release on completion of one half of the total sentence (section 1(1)), subject to the possibility of having "additional days" added to the sentence, either before or after the sentence is imposed, for breaches of prison discipline (section 24). Save in cases where the sentencing court has imposed at the time of sentence a "supervised release order" in terms of section 14 of the Act (see below), short term prisoners have no liability to supervision on release. They may, however, seek voluntary supervision under section 27(1)(c) of the Social Work (Scotland) Act 1968 (as amended by the Law Reform (Miscellaneous Provisions) (Scotland) Act 1990, section 61(4) (a)).

On release from custody, the only continuing liability in relation to the original sentence is to be ordered, on conviction of a further offence which is punishable by imprisonment, to be returned to prison for the whole or part of the original sentence which was outstanding on the date of commission of the subsequent offence (section 16). This power is available only in relation to persons released from sentences of imprisonment imposed directly on conviction of a criminal offence. Thus fine defaulters and those sentenced for contempt of court are not subject to the provision (section 5(1)). The order may be made in addition to or instead of any other order the court can make, but the court must, in Scotland, be of at least the same level as the original sentencing court. If the subsequent court is inferior to the original court, it may refer the case to the superior court in question (section 16(2)). Courts in England and Wales are similarly empowered to refer cases to the original sentencing court (section 16(3)). An order to continue serving the original sentence is appealable in the same way as any sentence of imprisonment, and the sentence may be ordered to be served before, after or concurrently with any other sentence imposed for the new offence (section 16(5)). If a new sentence of imprisonment of less than four years is imposed in addition to an order in relation to the original sentence, subsequent release from the new sentence will be on licence (section 16(7)). **06–20**

(i) Supervised release orders
Supervised release orders are a new sentence created by the 1993 Act and available for use when a court sentences someone to a period in custody of not less than 12 months but less than four years (section 212A of the 1975 Act, as inserted **06–21**

by section 14 of the 1993 Act). The orders are designed to "protect the public from serious harm from the offender on his release" and may last for a maximum of 12 months or the balance of the original prison sentence at the time of release. The imposition of a supervised release order does not require the consent of the offender, but it is appealable as part of the sentence of the court. The order will contain conditions requiring the person to be under the supervision of a local authority (or probation authority in England and Wales) and to comply with conditions specified to prevent or lessen the possibility of re-offending in any way. It is envisaged that these orders will be used for types of offender or offence where it is known that there is a high possibility of re-offending, and where community supervision can make a significant contribution to reducing this risk.

06–22   Persons subject to a supervised release order, or their supervisors, may apply to the Secretary of State to vary the authority responsible for supervision (section 15(1)–(3)). Additionally, they may apply to the court which made the order to have any of the terms varied, amended or cancelled or new terms added, subject to the same maximum period of duration as applied when the original order was made (section 15(4)–(6)).

06–23   Under section 16 of the Act, breach of a supervised release order may result in a court, on the application of the supervisor, the director of social work of the appropriate area or any officer appointed by him for the purpose, ordering the offender to be returned to prison for the whole or part of the period between the first proven breach of the order and the expiry of the order. The court also has power to vary the order in any way which would have been competent under section 15. Return to prison results in the order being terminated, even if re-release happens before the order would otherwise have expired (section 18(4)). No clear standard of proof is set down for establishing breaches of orders, but the evidence of one witness is sufficient (section 18(3)). A return to custody under section 18 is not a sentence for the purposes of this Act and the returned person therefore will not qualify for any reduction of this part of the sentence (section 18(5)). Appeals against decisions to vary supervised release orders or to impose a period of imprisonment for breach of an order are subject to the same time-limits as are generally applicable in relation to sentences (section 19).

(b) Long-term prisoners

(i) Ordinary release
Unless released earlier on parole, persons sentenced to four **06–24** years or more, either in a single sentence or as a result of cumulative sentences running partly or wholly consecutively, qualify for release on licence when they have served two-thirds of the total sentence (section 1(2)). Again the only matter which can delay this date is the award of "additional days" by a prison governor for breaches of prison discipline. Conditions of the licence will be determined by the Secretary of State after consultation with the parole board (section 12). He may also make rules for regulating the supervision of any person released on licence (section 13). These licences are a new imposition in Scotland. It is not clear what conditions they will contain, but their relationship to parole licences will be particularly interesting to observe. The persons to whom they will apply will not have been found worthy of parole and must therefore have been viewed as more of a risk to the community than those who are paroled. It might be expected, therefore, that the licences will be more restrictive than parole licences. Apart from the assessed risk argument, if the licences are less restrictive than parole licences, there might be little incentive for prisoners to seek parole for the one-sixth of the sentence for which it is available. At the same time, however, like the supervised release order discussed above, these licences will be imposed without the consent of the persons who are to be subject to them. Accordingly, there might be special difficulties in enforcing the conditions contained in them. Provisions for dealing with revocation of licence are the same as for parole licences.

Commission of a new offence punishable by **06–25** imprisonment in Scotland or in England or Wales during the period of licence renders the released person subject to the possibility of recall by a court in the same way, and subject to the same rules, as a short-term prisoner during the outstanding balance of his sentence.

(ii) Parole
Prisoners' eligibility. Long term prisoners are eligible for **06–26** consideration for parole under the 1993 Act (section 1(3)), unless they have been sentenced for non-payment of a fine or for contempt of court (section 5). The qualifying date for

consideration of parole is the date on which one-half of the total sentence has been served (section 1(3)), subject to the impact of any award of "additional days" under section 24 of the Act (section 27(6)). The 1993 Act makes several changes to the parole scheme in addition to this change in the minimum qualifying period.

06–27 *Constitution and function of the parole board.* The constitution of the board remains basically the same, though the new Act (Schedule 2, paragraph 2(a)) provides that the judicial member must be a Lord Commissioner of Justiciary, rather than a "person who holds or has held judicial office" under the 1989 Act. The board must, therefore, consist of a chairman, a Lord Commissioner of Justiciary, a registered medical practitioner who is a psychiatrist, a person appearing to the Secretary of State to have knowledge and experience of the supervision or after-care of discharged prisoners and a person appearing to the Secretary of State to have made a study of the causes of delinquency or the treatment of offenders, in addition to any others the Secretary of State may appoint. All appointments are made by the Secretary of State and may be renewed on expiry. The practice has been for appointments to be for three years, subject to renewal. Board members are paid a daily allowance. The board must submit an annual report on its work to the Secretary of State, and this report must be laid before Parliament (Schedule 2). There is no provision for the continuation of local review committees in the Act; accordingly, all cases will be considered by the board itself.

06–28 The main duty of the board is to advise the Secretary of State on matters referred to it by him under the Act in relation to the early release or recall of prisoners (section 20(2)). The Act does, however, provide that the Secretary of State may in effect delegate his responsibility for making the final release decision in relation to classes of case under the Act to the parole board (section 20(3)). It also empowers the Secretary of State to make rules regarding the proceedings of the board (section 20(4)), and to give directions on matters to be taken into account by the board in reaching its decisions (section 20(5)).

06–29 These powers have been exercised in the Parole Board (Scotland) Rules 1993 (1993 No. 2225 (S. 235)). Part IV of the Rules applies only to tribunal cases (which are dealt with separately below, under Discretionary Life Sentence Cases), but Part II applies to all cases, with the exceptions noted in the text below, and Part III applies only to non-tribunal cases. It should be borne in mind that, except where the contrary is stated, all of this only applies to persons sentenced to four years or more after October 1, 1993. The system for other prisoners remains as described above.

Part II Rules—applicable to all cases. Rule 4 requires that, **06–30** when the Secretary of State refers a case to the parole board for consideration of release of a prisoner, the prisoner must also be notified in writing. Not later than two weeks after the date of reference to the board, the Secretary of State must send to both the board and the prisoner a dossier containing any materials thought relevant to the case, and in particular the matters contained in the Schedule to the Rules (rule 5). In Part IV cases referred to the board before April 1, 1994, where the prisoner is a discretionary life sentence prisoner covered by paragraph 6 of Schedule 5 to the Act (*i.e.* sentenced before the introduction of the Act, but having had a "prescribed period" set for him by the Lord Justice General under the transitional powers granted by the Act), this time limit is extended to 12 weeks. The information to be sent includes the prisoner's record in prison, a detailed note of the offence for which he was sentenced and a record of previous offences and reports on the prisoner's circumstances and behaviour, and his suitability for release.

These provisions do not apply when the case is referred for **06–31** consideration of recall (rule 3(2)). It is not clear, therefore, what information must be revealed to the prisoner who has been recalled. In the (English) case of *R.* v. *Secretary of State for the Home Department, ex p. Singh, The Times,* April 27, 1993, Mr Singh sought and was granted judicial review of the English board's decision to recall him from licence after release from a sentence of detention during Her Majesty's pleasure and an order allowing him to see all the reports, subject to any claim for public interest immunity, which had been before the board when it made its decision. The Home Office had already decided to make available all reports to ordinary life-sentence prisoners as a matter of policy (*Hansard* Vol. 26, No. 97, col. 218–219). It might thus be presumed that the materials constituting the grounds for recall are not included in the rule 3 exemption.

In all other cases there is thus a general requirement that **06–32** all the information sent to the parole board or tribunal must be made available to the prisoner. However, provision is made in rule 6 for the Secretary of State not to disclose to the person concerned information which would be likely to be damaging on one or more of the following grounds:

>   (a) that it would be likely adversely to affect the health, welfare or safety of that person or any other person;
>   (b) that it would be likely to result in the commission of an offence;
>   (c) that it would be likely to facilitate an escape from legal custody or the doing of any act prejudicial to the safe keeping of persons in legal custody;
>   (d) that it would be likely to impede the prevention or detection of offences or the apprehension or prosecution of suspected offenders;
>   (e) that it would be likely otherwise to damage the public interest (rule 6(1)).

06–33   The person concerned must be informed in writing that such information has been sent to the board and given the heading under which it has not been divulged to him (rule 6(2)(c)). He must be told, as far as is practicable without prejudicing the reason for confidentiality, the gist or substance of the damaging information, and of his right to make representations about its non-disclosure. The board may then take this information into account (*ibid.*). This procedure does not apply in the case of discretionary life tribunals (see below).

06–34   On receipt of the dossier, the prisoner has four weeks to submit to the board, with copies to the Secretary of State, any representations in writing of his own or any other written information which he wishes the board to take into account (rule 7). No information in relation to the proceedings can be disclosed to any person not involved in the proceedings except insofar as the chairman of the board or tribunal may direct or in connection with any court proceedings (rule 9).

06–35   *Matters to be taken into account by the board.* Rule 8 provides a non-exhaustive list of matters to be taken into account by the board in dealing with cases. These are:

>   the nature and circumstances of any offence of which the person has been convicted or found guilty by a court;
>   the person's conduct since the date of his present sentence(s);
>   the likelihood of the person committing any offence or causing harm to any other person if he were to be

released on licence, remain on licence or be re-released on licence as the case may be;

the person's intentions on release, remaining at liberty or being re-released, and the likelihood of these intentions being fulfilled;

any written information, documents or written representations sent to the board by the Secretary of State or the prisoner, or otherwise obtained by the board.

Time. The parole board or the chairman of a tribunal is given discretion to vary the time allowed for the completion of any act under the Rules on application by either party, and time limits expiring on Saturdays, Sundays or public holidays are deemed to have been complied with if the act is done on the next lawful day (rule 10). The office of the board and the last known address of any other intended recipient are the addresses to which any document or material required or authorised by the Rules should be delivered or sent (rule 11). Irregularities resulting from failure to comply with any provisions of the Rules do not of themselves render the proceedings void. The board or the tribunal is empowered to give such directions as it thinks fit to cure or waive the irregularity and must give such directions when it considers that a person has been prejudiced by it. Clerical mistakes or errors arising in documents from accidental slips or omissions may be corrected by certificate under the hand of the relevant chairman (rule 12). **06–36**

Part III Rules—applicable only to non-tribunal cases. The quorum of the board for all purposes is set at three members (rule 14), though it is understood that the board generally intends to continue its practice of meeting as a full board in dealing with cases. The board is empowered to regulate its own procedure in dealing with cases, subject to the Rules. It must consider any written information, documents or written representations which the Secretary of State or the person being considered has submitted to it in terms of rules 5 and 7. It is also empowered to request and consider information from any other person and in any form (rule 15(4)). The Rules also provide, on the application of the person concerned, or where the board considers it desirable, for the chairman of the board to authorise one or two members to interview any person before a decision is taken (rule 15(3)). It is likely that this power will be used in effect to **06–37** replace the interview previously carried out by a member of the local review committee. Decisions by simple majority are sufficient, and the record is required to state whether the decision was unanimous or by majority. When the board is constituted by an even number, the chairman or presiding member has a casting vote (rule 16).

Part IV Rules (see below, under "discretionary life cases")

B. Indeterminate Sentences

1. Ordinary Life Sentence Prisoners

06–38   Section 1(4) of the 1993 Act re-enacts the existing provisions relating to the release of life sentence prisoners who are not "discretionary life prisoners". A "discretionary life prisoner" is defined by section 2 as a life prisoner whose sentence was imposed for an offence the sentence for which is not fixed by law and for whom an order has been made specifying a "relevant part" of the sentence (see below). In essence, therefore, all life-sentence prisoners sentenced on conviction of murder, whatever their age on conviction, and those others sentenced to life for whom a "relevant part" has not been set, are to be treated in basically the same way as before the Act, subject to the procedural changes outlined above in relation to the proceedings of the parole board. The main substantive changes relate to the discretionary lifers.

06–39   The only mechanism by which life sentence prisoners can be released from custody, apart from compassionate release under section 3 of the 1993 Act and exercise of the Royal Prerogative, is through the grant of release under licence. While this process involves the parole board and is very similar in many ways to parole of determinate sentence prisoners, the release is not known as parole but "release on licence".

(a) Review by the Secretary of State

06–40   The arrangements for ordinary lifers are normally that their cases are reviewed by the Secretary of State after roughly four years of the sentence have been completed. In practice this review is carried out by the Preliminary Review Committee (PRC), an informal committee established by the Secretary of State and consisting of civil servants, the chairman of the parole board, a psychiatrist, a High Court judge and a prison governor. The PRC takes into account reports on the prisoner's progress in custody, the trial judge's comments, if any, and the nature and quality of the offence of which the person was convicted. It makes a recommendation to the Secretary of State as to when the first review of the person's sentence for the purposes of release on licence should commence. Commonly this will be between the seventh and eighth year of the sentence, though special factors may lead to an earlier or later first review.

A recent series of English decisions relating to this **06–41** procedure may have some relevance to Scottish procedures, though the practice south of the border has been slightly different. There, judges submit a report on all life sentences when the sentence is passed, giving a recommendation as to the period to be served, and the Secretary of State consults the Lord Chief Justice and the trial judge in settling the date for the commencement of the first review. It has now been held (*R.* v. *Secretary of State for the Home Department, ex p. Doody* [1993] Q.B. 157) that the Secretary of State is obliged to reveal to the prisoner any opinion received from the judiciary as to the appropriate length of time to be served in custody. In addition, he must give the prisoner an opportunity to make in writing any representations the prisoner may wish in relation to the time which should be served for the purposes of retribution and deterrence. It had previously been established (*R.* v. *Secretary of State for the Home Department, ex p. Walsh, The Times,* December 18, 1991) that the Secretary of State should disclose to the prisoner the length of the tariff period applying to the prisoner. While Scottish judges may make recommendations in open court as to the minimum period a life sentence prisoner should serve before consideration for release, and such recommendations are appealable (1975 Act, section 205A), there is no authority for any informal recommendation and, it is submitted, any such recommendation should have no legal status. Prisoners are not currently invited to make representations at the stage of the decision about the timing of the first review, nor does it seem that the Secretary of State for Scotland operates a tariff system save in the case of those subject to the 1984 policy statement (see above). It is also established law in England and Wales that the Secretary of State is not bound by judicial recommendations (*Doody*) or, indeed, by any recommendation of the jury (*R.* v. *Secretary of State for the*

Home Department, ex p. Parker, The Times, October 6, 1992). Given that the Scottish Act requires only that the Secretary of State "consult" the judiciary, it is submitted that this is also the law in Scotland.

(b) Stages of Review

06–42   The Secretary of State makes the final decision about when the first formal review should start. It has been his practice to refer the case to the local review committee (LRC) as a first stage in the review. If the LRC recommends against release, the case is then normally referred to the parole board "for information only", *i.e.* with the implication that the Secretary of State would not contemplate release at that stage. The board may, of course, invite the Secretary of State to change his mind, but it has, and will continue to have, no authority to recommend release save in cases formally referred for consideration of release by the Secretary of State (section 1(5)). If, on the other hand, the LRC recommends a release programme on the review, the case is then assessed by officials of the Secretary of State. If they agree with the LRC, the case is sent to the Lord Justice-General and the trial judge, if still available, for their comments in terms of section 26(1) of the 1989 Act (section 1(4)(a) of the 1993 Act). The requirement is only that the Secretary of State should *consult* the judiciary—it is not necessary that their approval is obtained. No doubt, however, judicial opinion is given considerable weight and it is usually only when the judicial reaction is favourable that the case is then considered by the Secretary of State himself. If he too approves of the release, the case is sent to the board with a provisional programme leading to release after a period of preparation, usually in 18 months' to two years' time. The board then considers the case, normally interviewing the prisoner if it considers that the programme is feasible, and reaches a final decision on its recommendation. A positive recommendation from the board is required before the person can be released on licence (section 1(3)). If the case fails at any of the stages, it may be referred to the parole board on a "for information only" basis, again allowing the board to request reconsideration, but not allowing it to recommend a release programme.

06–43   It is not clear what pattern will be followed when the LRCs go out of existence. The one change in the law is a minor one—allowing the Lord Justice-Clerk to substitute for the

Lord Justice-General in the consultation process (section 1(4)(a)). It may be that the most rational process would be for the parole board to see all the cases at the stage where the LRCs have been seeing them and to make a recommendation on release before any of the other consultation takes place. The Secretary of State still retains the discretion about when cases should be referred in the first instance, and the ultimate decision about release even when the board has recommended release. He may, therefore, decide to continue the policy announced in 1984 whereunder persons sentenced to life imprisonment for the murder of police officers, murder by terrorists, sexual or sadistic murders of children or murder by firearm in the commission of crime, would not normally be granted release on licence until they had served at least 20 years in custody. The position continues as before, that the board's approval is a necessary but not sufficient condition to be fulfilled before a life sentence prisoner can be released.

(c) On Licence For Life

On release, life sentence prisoners remain on licence for life. **06–44** The licence contains the same standard conditions as a parole licence, and other conditions may be added by the Secretary of State on the recommendation of the parole board, as with determinate sentence prisoners. In a recent change of policy, however, the Secretary of State has decided that the requirement to be subject to supervision may be removed from a life licence after the person has been trouble free in the community for a period of 10 years. Removal of the supervision requirement requires an application to the board from the supervising officer, agreed to by a superior officer and the life licensee. Approval of the application does not remove subsequent liability to recall if any of the other terms of the licence are breached.

Procedure on breach of licence is the same as that adopted **06–45** in the case of determinate sentence parolees. A life licensee whose licence is revoked and who is not immediately ordered to be re-released by the parole board resumes serving the life sentence. Re-release then requires the same processes to be gone through, including the consultation with the judiciary, as the original release. Accordingly, recall is a serious step and can result in substantial additional time being spent in custody.

2. Discretionary Life Prisoners

06–46   Although life imprisonment is a sentence available for many crimes, it has not commonly been used by Scottish courts for crimes other than murder. It is thought that there are currently some 36 persons serving life imprisonment whose main offence is other than murder. Traditional practice has been to treat them in exactly the same way as other lifers when considering their release on licence. As a result of cases before the European Court of Human Rights brought by English prisoners serving discretionary life sentences, this has had to change.

06–47   In *Thyne, Wilson and Gunnell* v. *U.K.* (Series A, No. 190–A, ECHR) the applicants, three discretionary life sentence prisoners, complained that there was no mechanism by which they could challenge their continued detention after the period which the sentencing court had specified as the "tariff period" for the offences of which they were convicted. English courts are in the habit of specifying such a period, representing the determinate sentence which the judge would have considered appropriate for the offence if a life sentence had not been imposed. The European Court of Human Rights held that discretionary life-sentence prisoners have the right to have their release dates determined by a judicial process once they have served the tariff period. The U.K. government has accepted this ruling and implemented a new system in England and Wales under the Criminal Justice Act 1991.

06–48   While it has not been judicial practice to make similar recommendations in Scotland, or, indeed, for the judges often to use their formal powers under section 205A of the 1975 Act to make minimum recommendations in life sentence cases (for a discussion of the factors to be taken into account in making such recommendations and an opinion on what the minimum such recommendation should be, see *Casey* v. *H.M. Advocate*, 1994 S.L.T. 54), it has been considered wise to adopt a similar procedure in relation to discretionary life sentences as has been adopted in England.

(a) New Procedure

06–49   Section 2 of the 1993 Act requires a court in imposing a discretionary life sentence to address the question of whether it should specify a period to be served before the prisoner can insist that his case is referred to the parole board for consideration of release and before the board can direct the Secretary of State to release the person. If the court decides not to specify a "relevant part", as the period is to be known in Scotland, it must give reasons for not doing so. Any decision in relation to a relevant part, including the decision not to specify one, is subject to appeal in the same way as any other sentence. In setting the relevant part, the court is obliged to take into account the seriousness of the offence and any offences related to it and any previous convictions of the person. There are, however, no guidelines as to when a discretionary life sentence itself is appropriate.

The provision is retroactive in cases considered appropriate. Schedule 5, paragraph 6 of the 1993 Act requires the Secretary of State, in consultation with the Lord Justice-General and the trial judge, if available, to review the cases of all prisoners already under discretionary life sentences on October 1, 1993, and to consider whether, if section 2 had been in force at the time of sentence, an order would have been made under it and, if so, what order. The new procedure then applies immediately to all cases for which a relevant part is set either by the court or under these transitional arrangements. **06–50**

Discretionary life sentence prisoners for whom a relevant part has been set have different rights from other life sentence prisoners in relation to the determination of their release dates. In the first place, the parole board has the power to *order* (as opposed to recommend) the release of such prisoners once the Secretary of State has referred the case to it (section 2(4)). There is no role in the process for the judiciary, and the Secretary of State must comply with the order of the board. Secondly, the prisoner, having served the relevant part specified by the court or under the transitional arrangements, may require the Secretary of State to refer the case to the parole board at any time, and thereafter at not less than intervals of two years from any previous referral (section 2(6) and (7)(b)). If the discretionary life-sentence prisoner is also serving another sentence or sentences, the normal requirements for consideration of parole must be met in relation to such sentence or sentences before the case can be considered under these provisions (section 2(7)(a) and (9)). **06–51**

Before issuing a directive to the Secretary of State to release such a prisoner, the board must be satisfied that it is no longer necessary for the protection of the public that the person be confined (section 2(5)(b)). In conformity with the European Court of Human Rights judgment, the board is **06–52** constituted as a court in dealing with these cases. Accordingly, the hearings are to be markedly different from other parole board hearings, and are governed by Part IV of the Parole Board (Scotland) Rules 1993.

(b) Hearings Under Part IV of the Parole Board (Scotland) Rules 1993

06–53   For the purposes of dealing with these cases, the chairman of the parole board is empowered to appoint three members of the board to form a tribunal (rule 18(1)). One of the appointed members must hold or have held judicial office, and that person shall be appointed chairman of the tribunal (rule 18(2)). Provision is made to cater for the death, incapacity or unavailability of any tribunal member in the normal way (rule 18(3)).

06–54   Subject to the Rules, the tribunal is responsible for regulating its own procedure (rule 19(1)). The chairman may give, vary or revoke directions for the conduct of the case in relation to the timetable for proceedings, the time limits imposed by the Rules, the service of documents, and the submission of evidence, at the chairman's own motion or on the written application of either party, notice of which must be given to the other party. Both parties must be given an opportunity to make written representations on these directions or allowed to make oral submissions at a preliminary hearing (rule 19(2)(3)). Rule 6 of the Parole Board Rules does not apply to Part IV cases. Accordingly, the prisoner cannot be denied access to any of the papers which are submitted to the tribunal.

(i) Preliminary hearing

06–55   The chairman of the tribunal may decide to order a preliminary hearing in regard to any matter and must give at least 14 days notice of such a hearing to the parties (rule 19(4)). The hearing shall be held in private, with nothing made public unless otherwise ordered by the chairman (rule 19(5)). The chairman sits alone at preliminary hearings and both parties and their representatives may attend (rule 19(6)). Decisions about directions must be issued and copied to both parties as soon as practicable after any preliminary hearing (rule 19(7)).

(ii) Full hearing

06–56   *Notice.* Rule 20 requires that there be an oral hearing of the prisoner's case unless both parties and the tribunal agree otherwise. The tribunal must give the parties at least three week's notice of the hearing, unless both parties agree to shorter notice (rule 21(1)). Again unless both parties agree otherwise, the hearing shall not take place less than three weeks from the end of the period within which the prisoner may send in written representations in terms of rule 7 (rule 21(2)). Any notice of a hearing may be varied on not less than seven days notice (rule 21(3)). Hearings may be adjourned, with no further notice being required when the date, time and place of the adjourned hearing are given at the time of the adjournment, and not less than seven days notice in other cases (rule 21(4)).

Representation. Parties may authorise anyone to represent them at a hearing (rule 22(1)), subject to the tribunal's discretion, for good and sufficient reasons, to refuse to permit a person to represent a party (rule 22(2)). Parties are required to submit the name, address and occupation of any representative to the tribunal within the same time-limit as that established for the prisoner to submit written representations (not less than four weeks from the date of receipt of the dossier by the prisoner) (rule 22(2)). The tribunal, with the agreement of the party, may appoint a representative to act for that party when the party has not authorised anyone to act on his behalf (rule 22(4)). Schedule 4, paragraph 4 to the 1993 Act added a new section 21(1)(aa) to the Legal Aid (Scotland) Act 1986 to permit the grant of legal aid for any case referred under section 2(6) of the 1993 Act. **06–57**

Witnesses. Parties wishing to call witnesses at the hearing must make written application to the tribunal no later than four weeks after the dossier has been sent to the prisoner (rule 23(1)). The application must outline, in addition to the name, address and occupation of each witness, the general nature of the evidence the person is likely to supply (rule 23(2)). A copy of the application must be sent to the other party (rule 23(3)). The chairman of the tribunal will determine the application and give notice of his decision, with reasons when he refuses the application, to both parties (rule 23(4)). Similar provisions apply if either party wishes to be accompanied to a hearing by any person in addition to a representative (rule 24). **06–58**

Attendance. Hearings are to be held in private (rule 25(1)). Only members of, and the clerk to, the tribunal, the parties and their representatives, witnesses and other persons **06–59** authorised by the chairman or by the tribunal and members of the Council of Tribunals or of the Scottish Committee of that Council are allowed to attend hearings (rule 25(2)(4)). Both the Secretary of State and the person responsible for the security of any building in which a hearing takes place may apply to the chairman if they consider that it is necessary, in the interests of the security of the building or the safety of any person attending the hearing, for any person or persons to be present in addition to the others at the hearing. The chairman has discretion in relation to such applications, but must inform parties of his decision, and the reasons for any refusal to allow this (rule 25(3)).

06–60   *Procedure.* At the beginning of the hearing, the chairman must explain the order of proceedings to be adopted (rule 26(1)). Formality in the proceedings should be avoided as far as is compatible with the clarification of the issues to be decided and just handling of the proceedings (rule 26(2)). The parties may be heard in whatever order the tribunal determines, and are entitled to be heard in person or through their representative, to hear each other's evidence and that of the witnesses, and to put questions to anyone giving evidence; to call authorised witnesses and to make submissions to the tribunal (rule 26(3)). Members of the tribunal are also allowed to put questions to any party, representative or witness (see above). Persons whose conduct has disrupted or, in the opinion of the tribunal, is likely to disrupt, the hearing may be excluded from the hearing (rule 26(4)). The hearing may consider any document or information, even if it would be inadmissible in a court of law, but it cannot compel the giving of evidence or production of documents which could not be compelled in proceedings before a court (rule 26(5)).

06–61   *Decision.* Majority decisions by a tribunal are acceptable, with the chairman having a casting vote if the tribunal is constituted by two persons. The decision must record whether the decision was unanimous or by majority (rule 27(1)). The parties must be sent a written copy of the decision and reasons for the decision within 14 days of the hearing (rule 27(2)).

(c) Other Matters in Relation to Discretionary Life Prisoners

06–62   If the tribunal decides to issue a directive to the Secretary of State to release the prisoner, the release should take place as soon as possible. The prisoner will be subject to a licence on release with the conditions of the licence, and any subsequent variation of the conditions, specified by the parole board (1993 Act, section 12(3)(a)). With other parole and life licences, the Secretary of State is only required to consult the board before imposing or varying a licence condition. In discretionary life cases, however, only the parole board can impose or vary licence conditions, and the Secretary of State has no power to act on his own.

The licence stays in force for the rest of the person's life, **06–63** unless it is revoked earlier. Breach of any of the terms of the licence may give rise to the same procedures as breach of an ordinary life licence (see above), and presumably the same practice will be followed in relation to cancelling the supervision requirement after a period of 10 years in the community without adverse reports.

Compassionate Release

Section 3 of the 1993 Act applies to all persons serving a **06–64** sentence of imprisonment. It empowers the Secretary of State to release any prisoner on licence at any time when he is satisfied that there are compassionate grounds for so doing. If the circumstances make it practicable, he must consult the parole board before exercising this discretion in the case of a person sentenced to four years or more (section 3(2)), but the consent of the board is not required in any case.

The Act offers no definition of "compassionate", nor any **06–65** appeal mechanism against a decision of the Secretary of State. On the basis of the parliamentary discussion of the provision, it is envisaged that the power will be used sparingly and in extreme cases. Thus it may be used to release prisoners at the final stage of a terminal illness, so ensuring, as far as possible, that no one dies in custody. It does not replace the Royal Prerogative of Mercy, the common law power of the Crown to order the release of anyone at any time. It does have the advantage over the Royal Prerogative that release will be on licence, allowing the prisoner to be recalled if, for example, a seemingly terminal illness is subsequently cured or significantly remitted.

Section 17 of the Act empowers the Secretary of State to **06–66** recall a person released under section 3. If the person is a long-term prisoner (*i.e.* sentenced to four years or more) or a life-sentence prisoner, the recall can be ordered by the parole board or by the Secretary of State when consultation with the board is not practicable. In relation to short-term prisoners, the power of recall belongs to the Secretary of State alone and may be exercised when he is satisfied that the person's health or circumstances have so changed that were he in prison his release under section 3(1) would no longer be justified. In all cases a recalled person has the right to be told on his return to prison the reasons for the recall and of his right to make written representations to the Secretary of State about it. All long term prisoners who are recalled by the Secretary of State without the involvement of the parole board, and all who are recalled on the recommendation of the board, and who choose to make written representations against their recall, have the right to have their cases referred to the board. The board may then order the immediate re-release of the person, and the Secretary of State must comply with such an order from the board (section 17(4)). Short-term prisoners released under section 3 have no access to the parole board (section 17(1)(b)). Release under section 3 will not activate any supervised release order which may have been imposed under section 14 of the 1993 Act.

Royal Prerogative of Mercy

06–67 The Crown retains the privilege at all times of exercising the prerogative of mercy in relation to anyone in prison. The effect of the exercise of this prerogative is that the person is immediately released and is under no further liability in relation to the sentence. It does not amount to an acquittal, but neither is the person liable to recall to custody for the offence for which the prerogative was exercised. It is, of course, rarely used.

Provisions Affecting Released Prisoners

1. Rehabilitation of Offenders Act 1974

06–68 To assist at least some ex-prisoners on release from prison, the law provides for the convictions which led to imprisonment to become spent in certain circumstances. The Act does not apply to any sentence of imprisonment or detention of over 30 months (including life imprisonment, detention during Her Majesty's Pleasure and detention without limit of time). Otherwise, subject to the exceptions explained below, and provided that the person is not convicted of any other offence during the period, a conviction leading to a sentence of over six months becomes spent after 10 years, in the case of a person 21 years or older on conviction, and five years in the case of a person below that age. A sentence of six months or less attracts a rehabilitation period of seven years for an adult and three and a half years for a young offender. Commission of another offence during the rehabilitation period causes the period of rehabilitation to start again for the new conviction.

The effect of the Act is that a person who has been **06–69** rehabilitated in accordance with the above definition must be treated, for most purposes, as if he had not committed, or been charged with, or prosecuted for, or convicted of, or sentenced for, the offence(s) which was the subject of that conviction (section 4(1)). It is in the field of gaining employment that the Act is of perhaps most use. Thus a person who qualifies under the Act does not have to disclose any spent conviction when applying for a job and cannot be fairly dismissed for having failed to do so. There are, however, many exceptions to the Act, contained in the Rehabilitation of Offenders Act 1974 (Exceptions) Order 1975. In essence, any post which is in the medical (including veterinary medicine) or dental, legal, educational, accountancy or military world, as well as any post which involves working with children or the disabled, is exempt from the Act, and full disclosure must be made.

2. Firearms Act 1968

Persons sentenced to three years or more in detention or **06–70** prison are permanently banned from possessing a firearm or ammunition (section 21(1)). Those sentenced to between three months but less than three years are prohibited from possessing firearms and ammunition for a period of five years commencing from the date of leaving prison (section 21(2)). In both cases the person may apply to a sheriff to have the prohibition lifted (section 23(6)).

3. Jury Service

Persons who have been sentenced anywhere in the British **06–71** Isles to a period of five years or more in custody are excluded from jury service for life. Equally, anyone who has served any part of any sentence of imprisonment or detention in the last 10 years is excluded from such service.

Comments on the Parole System

06–72   A review of the arrangements for the early release of prisoners was carried out in Scotland in 1988/89 by a committee appointed by the Secretary of State under the chairmanship of Lord Kincraig. The basic philosophy underlying the recommendations of the committee's report (*Parole and Related Issues in Scotland* Cm. 598 (1989)), was that each part of a custodial sentence imposed by a court should have a real meaning. The system of remission, it was felt, effectively discounted one-third of every sentence and detracted from public understanding of the sentencing process. Equally, the parole system could result in a person with a three-year sentence being released before someone with a two-year sentence, and was felt by some not to operate in accordance with the principles of natural justice.

06–73   The committee rejected suggestions that parole should be abolished. It was felt that a system of parole enabled account to be taken of changes in a person subsequent to sentence, or in the information available about that person, which made it possible for the person to be released without undue risk to the community. Accordingly, the committee recommended that parole should continue to be available, though it suggested that, to allow changes to happen and be perceived by those reporting on the prisoner, the minimum sentence eligible for parole should be five years. For sentences under that period, the committee recommended that release be granted when one-half of the sentence had been served, but that conviction for another offence punishable by imprisonment on indictment during the release period should lead to the automatic recall of the person to serve the balance of the sentence outstanding at the date of commission of the new offence. This would ensure that every part of a sentence of imprisonment had at least some impact, but without requiring the person to serve every day of the sentence in custody.

06–74   The committee also suggested a review of parole procedures and documentation and, by a majority, that prisoners be allowed access to all the reports considered by the parole board. Rule 5 of the Parole Board Rules implements this majority recommendation, but the review of procedures and documentation did not necessitate any legislative intervention. Rather, the parole board itself, along with Scottish Office civil servants and SPS officials, has begun to address the identified problems.

Two particular areas are being tackled. First, the contents **06–75** of the dossiers on which decisions are made are being reviewed. A new dossier is being piloted in two establishments. It attempts to separate "factual" information from opinion in all reports and to cut down on duplication within the dossier. Originally it had been planned to allow prisoners access to the factual section for checking, but, at the insistence of prison staff, the reports which they write are also being made available to the prisoner for his comments. Thus, when the legal requirement to allow prisoners to see dossiers begins to apply under the 1993 Rules, there will already have been considerable experience of at least the prison produced part having been available to the prisoners.

Secondly, the board is moving towards providing written **06–76** reasons for all decisions directly to prisoners. The board has never been satisfied that the existing arrangement, whereby a minute of the board's discussion is sent to the prison and prison staff are encouraged to use it in counselling the prisoner, actually worked in all cases. In any event, it seems much more logical for the decision to be communicated directly to the person concerned. This change, however, requires additional administrative support for the board, but it is thought that it will proceed as soon as resources are made available.

The 1993 Act adopts the majority of the Kincraig **06–77** Committee's other recommendations. The Act puts calculation of release dates on a much more rational footing and achieves the objective of giving meaning to the whole of the original sentence. By opening up the parole sentence to greater involvement by the prisoner, especially by ensuring that he sees all the information on which the decisions are to be based, it may also produce more judicial challenges to decisions taken regarding the grant, or refusal of parole and to recall decisions. If such challenges produce a more just system, they can only be welcomed by all involved.

The provision for tribunals for discretionary life-sentence **06–78** prisoners in Scotland closely mirrors the provision made south of the border, where they have now had some experience of hearings. Initial results have not been that the tribunals have ordered many immediate releases, but they have made suggestions about the management of the prisoners to improve their prospects of moving towards release. Experience will build fairly rapidly in Scotland, as the tribunals deal with the cases of prisoners already on sentence who are given a "prescribed period" by the transitional provisions of the Act. After this initial flurry, the number of cases will rapidly diminish in Scotland.

06–79   It is envisaged that the hearings will normally take place in the institution in which the prisoner is detained. Preliminary hearings, to deal with applications in relation to witnesses and written and documentary submissions, may take place at the board's headquarters, but care will be taken not to exclude the attendance of parties at any part of the process if this would be a breach of natural justice. In all other aspects the tribunal will function like any other, and the availability of legal aid makes clear the commitment to ensure that parties are properly represented at the hearings.

06–80   In many ways, especially by allowing the attendance of the person whose case is being discussed, these hearings reflect the normal practice for all parole proceedings in other parts of the world, notably Canada and the U.S. Scotland has rejected that model of decision-making for parole decisions in general, and has introduced the tribunal procedure only as a result of pressure from the European Court of Human Rights. It may be that there will be continuing pressure from that source to extend the court-like apparatus to other cases, first, perhaps, to other indeterminate sentences and subsequently to all parole decisions. However, the new openness in relation to the materials which the board considers in reaching decisions in all parole cases, and the direct contact the applicant for parole will have with a board member or members, may reduce it. The changes introduced by the 1993 Act and the Rules, allied with the review of dossier contents undertaken within the Scottish Office and the move towards providing reasoned decisions on parole applications directly to the prisoners, should ensure not only an improvement in procedural justice but also a substantive improvement in decision-making. All of this should improve the perception of the parole system in the eyes of prisoners and society.

CHAPTER 7

CONCLUSIONS AND PROJECTIONS

Pressures for Change

The Prisons and Young Offenders Institutions (Scotland) **07–01**
Rules 1994 may mark the end of an era. In form and in
substance, they bring together the developments which have
taken place in penological theory, in domestic and
international legal thinking and in managerial practice in
Scotland. Previous developments in the inherently
conservative world of the prison have not required
significant change in the form of the law. The similarities
between the Prisons (Scotland) Acts of 1877 and 1989, and
the fact that the 1952 Rules reigned without substantial
amendment throughout a period of over 40 years, make that
point clear. But the old form had become incapable of
supporting the new demands—demands made by prisoners,
by prison management, by the courts and by our
international treaty obligations. "Norms and substratum
have become so dissimilar, so incommensurable" (Renner,
The Institutions of Private Law and their Social Function, p. 290),
that one had to change.

The pressure for change had been relatively well **07–02**
controlled for a long time. The reasons for this control, and
the techniques by which it was achieved, were, insofar as
they were consciously addressed at all, seen as essential parts
of a prison system. Any idea of the substantive law according
rights to prisoners was virtually inconceivable at the time
when the legal structure was being established. "Outlawry",
with the consequent total loss of legal personality, was the
natural parent of imprisonment. Many vestiges of this
thinking are still evident in popular views of imprisonment
today. Deprivation of freedom is seen by many as implying
denial of anything perceived as more than a bare minimum.
The nineteenth century notion of "lesser eligibility", which
required the prison (and the workhouse) to provide inmates
with less of everything than the poorest "free" man, may
have been replaced by the rhetoric of "prison *as*, and not *for*,
punishment", but this has not stopped regular complaints
about any comforts being provided for prisoners.

141

Maintaining a regime of anything other than hard labour and strict religious observance—all in total silence, of course—was an enlightened breakthrough of the twentieth century. The Elgin Report of 1900 (*Report from the Departmental Committee on Scottish Prisons*, Cmnd. 218), Scotland's equivalent of the Gladstone Report of 1895 in England, which prompted this breakthrough, was in the vanguard of penal developments. But in many ways it was the last big initiative in Scotland until the late 1980s, and it required no change in the law. In the absence of a tradition which allowed the courts to challenge legislation, the silence of the statutes and statutory instruments on the matter of prisoners' rights was, until the last 20 years, definitive.

07–03   In addition, prisoners' access to the outside world was severely restricted, both physically and legally, by the very system which they were most likely to want to challenge. Without clearly enforceable legal rights, it was probably irrelevant that access to the courts was difficult for prisoners. But access was only available through visits, which were at the discretion of the authorities, and letters, which were subject to censorship. Effectively rendered voiceless, prisoners had to rely on outside groups advocating on their behalf. In an excellent study of pressure group activity in the area of penal reform, Ryan (*The Acceptable Pressure Group* (1978)) provides one explanation of why such groups are unlikely to be able to prompt radical reform. To be successful in securing change, a pressure group has to have access, formally and, perhaps more importantly, informally, to the power holders; it must be able to persuade them that its case is right and that there is broad support for it. The "respectable" group is likely to have easier access to power holders than prisoners and their friends, who are not likely to have social contacts with influential people or to have easy access to them through formal structures. Equally, access to knowledge about prisons is also controlled, with the "respectable" more likely to be allowed free reign within establishments to obtain information. Finance enters the equation too, with better-off groups more able to accumulate information, organise it, and present it in a convincing way, than the less-well-off groups. Prisoners and ex-prisoners are clearly knowledgeable about some aspects of imprisonment, but their knowledge is likely to be limited to what they have experienced. Few others, certainly among the power holders, share the experience or view it in the same way. Without more general or more acceptable knowledge, and the ability to present it in the accepted way, these groups are unlikely to be able to produce a persuasive case. Thus the voices which are heard are those which do not challenge the structures behind the systems; radical voices are effectively silenced.

Foreseeable Developments

Change, therefore, has been slow in coming and even slower **07–04** in being reflected in the law. The pressures which eventually caused the change are discussed in Chapter 1, and the law itself is as described in the remaining chapters of this book. The new situation is radically different from all that has gone before. The philosophy of the "responsible prisoner" will take time to be reflected in all the practices of the prison system; equally, it will take time for the new Rules and directions to settle into a final form. They will, no doubt, be tested through court action with a speed and a frequency with which their predecessors did not have to cope. But the basic structures are now established and should provide the framework for foreseeable developments, in at least the medium term.

No one can predict what the longer term developments are **07–05** likely to be. While our great-grandparents may have been amazed at the enormous amounts of money we spend locking people up, our great-grandchildren might consider that we were totally barbaric, as well as hopelessly misguided, in considering that we could tackle the problem of crime by taking offenders away from the community, depriving the (mostly) already deprived of choices and responsibilities, and expecting them to re-emerge into our community able to "live a good and useful life".

Medium term developments are more predictable, **07–06** perhaps especially in relation to the law in the international forum. The course for the domestic courts is reasonably well laid out, albeit by our southern neighbours. The number of cases arising from Scottish prisons is currently growing, and this trend will at least continue under the new Rules. But such developments can only be restricted to ensuring that these Rules are followed and that the rules of natural justice are observed in the process. Accordingly, while changes from this source will enhance the legal protection of prisoners, perhaps especially in relation to procedures at adjudications and those for deciding matters like security categories, parole eligibility and the allocation of privileges, it would be unrealistic to expect significant challenges to the system to emerge in this forum. Such challenges are likely, however, from the European Commission and other international bodies.

07–07   One of the strengths of the ECHR is that it has not been allowed to become an ossified set of rules. The mechanisms for interpretation and application of the Convention have ensured that the individuals who perform these tasks, in the Commission, the Council of Ministers and the court, all bring to the task the standards of their own jurisdictions. As standards have developed in member countries, at different rates and according to different philosophies and other constraints and prompts, the changes have been reflected in the judgments emerging from Strasbourg. It could have happened that the Convention became a method of imposing a lowest common denominator. But, consistent with the spirit of the enterprise, it has, instead, become a powerful force for improvements in the protection of the rights enshrined in the Convention. It is not likely that this will change. We can, therefore, look at what is already happening in other member states in relation to imprisonment to see the areas in which further legal challenges to Scottish practice have most chance of success.

07–08   Two such areas which spring easily to mind are overcrowding and physical conditions within prisons. At present, the Commission and the court are reluctant to hold that physical conditions short of those constituting sensory deprivation qualify as "inhuman or degrading treatment or punishment" under article 3 of the Convention. However, several member states (notably Holland and Ireland) are strict in their adherence to maximum numbers which can be detained in each of their establishments. In contrast, Scottish prisons are not allowed to refuse any prisoner sent to them with a valid warrant or committal order from a court. Consequently, there is no legally enforceable maximum number which each prison can hold, and prisons which receive people directly from courts often find themselves holding well over the numbers for which they were designed. Thus, at the time of writing, Barlinnie, Edinburgh, Inverness, Aberdeen and Dumfries—all receiving prisons for adult males in Scotland—are over their official capacity, with Aberdeen holding 140 per cent of its capacity. When even the official figures say that there are too many people in the building, it would not be surprising if a court with the power to rule on the question were to hold that crushing people into too small a space constituted degrading treatment.

The same may well be said about toilet and washing **07–09** facilities. Most of Scotland's penal estate was built at a time when the population was not, perhaps, so aware of the requirements of proper hygiene. But, as all residential properties in the outside world have had internal sanitation provided as a matter of course for several decades, and as it has no longer become odd to have more than one bath or shower a week, prisons have been left far behind with facilities designed for another age. It is difficult to imagine domestic courts being able to do anything about the lamentable position in many prisons (though perhaps the spread of an infectious disease in these conditions might lead to successful actions based on breach of duty of care or negligence), but it is the kind of area where progress may be encouraged through adverse European Court of Human Rights decisions.

Quasi-Legal Developments

1. The European Convention for the Prevention of Torture

The Council of Europe has not, however, rested on its laurels **07–10** and left the enforcement mechanism established under the original human rights convention to carry all the responsibility for enforcing proper respect for human rights in prisons. Rather, in the Convention for the Prevention of Torture, Inhuman or Degrading Treatment or Punishment ("the CPT"), the Council has created a proactive mechanism for assisting member states to comply with article 3 of the Human Rights Convention. Under the CPT, drafted in 1987 and opened for signature in 1989, member states agree to allow delegations from the committee formed to enforce the Convention to visit the member states and to have full and free access to any facility used for the detention of people deprived of their liberty for any reason. (This includes prisons, police stations, psychiatric hospitals and schools and other places where people may be held against their will.)

07–11   The primary aim of the CPT is, as its name suggests, to prevent violations of article 3. In doing this, however, the committee does not restrict itself to the fairly narrow interpretation of article 3 adopted by the European Court of Human Rights. Where the court and the Commission have required applicants to allege actual torture, or conditions so inimicable to the maintenance of human life and dignity as to constitute extremely inhuman or degrading treatment or punishment before they will find that there has been a breach of the article, the CPT has adopted a much broader interpretation of the article. It certainly looks for evidence of torture, as this would normally be understood, but it also sets a higher standard than the Court and Commission in its expectations of the physical conditions of detention and the facilities and regime activities available to detainees.

07–12   The CPT also has the advantage of conducting regular visits, as well as extraordinary ones in response to particular information received, rather than having to rely on individual applications like the ECHR and other court based systems. It can thus approach its task in a systematic way, and, with its rights of access, overcome any possible barriers which might be put in the way of individuals wishing to mount challenges to the state which is detaining them. It makes use of information from a variety of sources, official and unoffical, before, during and after its visits, and has access to all persons, places and records during its visits.

07–13   Each member state has the right to nominate a representative for election to the committee. Member states are encouraged to nominate people with a knowledge of and interest in issues relating to detention. Thus the committee regularly includes members who are legally or medically qualified, and people who have had relevant work experience in detention facilities. Members selected for individual visits, who cannot be nationals of the country to be visited, are accompanied on the visits by "expert advisers", usually two in number, with one being medically qualified (usually a psychiatrist) and the other experienced in penological matters. These experts are appointed on an *ad hoc* basis, to assist during a particular visit and to provide a written report to aid the committee in drafting its final report. In addition, the committee is served by a full-time secretariat, mostly legally qualified, who assist in preparation for visits, in maintaining databases on detention facilities and the rules regulating them, in the visiting process itself, in the preparation of reports, and in continuing negotiations with the countries visited.

All of the committee's work is carried out in a confidential way, and great stress is put on the need for member states to co-operate with the CPT. Member states are given advance notice of periodic visits, though special visits can be made without prior warning. The notice specifies which institutions the committee proposes to visit, but the committee retains, and commonly uses, its power to visit institutions not notified in advance. Members of the committee meet with officials, staff of institutions and detainees, and all such meetings are confidential. At the end of the visit, the committee meets again with officials to provide an indication of the areas of concern and, usually, to seek further information on any relevant matters. The committee may also use this opportunity to raise any matters of immediate concern and to ask for immediate remedial action to be taken in any area where the committee considers there is a need for such action. **07–14**

After the visit, the visiting members of the committee draw up a report for consideration by the whole committee in a plenary session. When this is adopted, it is sent to the government of the member state along with an invitation to the government to reply, within six months, to any of the observations made. The committee's intention is that the report should be the start of a dialogue between it and the member state, calculated to remedy any deficiency found and to ensure developments in harmony with the general aim of the CPT. Accordingly, both the report and the responses are confidential and remain so unless the member state involved agrees to publication. Only when the member state either refuses to co-operate in the resolution of any problems identified, or where it publishes any part of the committee's report without publishing the whole, can the committee proceed to publication of anything in relation to the visit, apart from the fact that it has taken place, without the member state's approval. So far the power to publish anything without the consent of the state involved has only been used on one occasion (see *Statement on Turkey* CPT, 1992). **07–15**

The majority of reports on visits so far carried out have been published with the full consent of the member states involved and along with a reply from the member state. A good example of the committee's work is the report on the **07–16**

visit to the U.K., published, along with the U.K. government's initial response, in 1992. A subsequent further
response, evidencing the on-going nature of the dialogue
established, was published in 1993. The committee found
that prison conditions observed during its visit (which did
not include any Scottish establishments) constituted
inhuman and degrading treatment, in particular in their
denial of proper access to sanitary facilities and in the degree
of overcrowding witnessed in local prisons. The U.K.
government's response included an undertaking to install
integral sanitation in prison cells by 1995 and to attempt to
eradicate overcrowding by the provision of new prison
places as soon as possible. These were both commitments
already made within the domestic political environment, but
the fact that they are now reiterated in response to an
international treaty body should help to ensure that they are
kept.

07–17   The CPT plans to visit each member state for periodic
visits on a three-year cycle. In addition, it carries out special
visits to check that commitments made are being kept. Each
member state has experienced at least one visit, and the
second U.K. visit, made in early summer 1994, included
establishments in Scotland. The report on this visit should be
available to the government by the end of 1994. By a protocol
to the Treaty opened for signature in 1993, states which are
not members of the Council of Europe are allowed to accede
to the Treaty. It is thought likely that many states of the
former Soviet Union will use this opportunity to obtain
assistance to develop their detention facilities in conformity
with the standards obtaining in the rest of Europe.

07–18   Such voluntary acceptance of the jurisdiction of the CPT,
by both members and non-members of the Council of
Europe, is a clear indication of international perceptions of
the importance of securing decent conditions and proper
protection for detainees. The CPT has already become an
important force for change in this area and, as its standards
develop, it is likely to grow in its influence—in Scotland as
much as in the rest of Eruope. While treaty obligations form
no part of our domestic law, they are nonetheless crucial in
motivating political action, and it is unlikely that the U.K.
government would wish to be seen to be in breach of the
standards imposed by this particular treaty. Accordingly,
the CPT is likely to be very influential in the U.K. specifically
in the areas, like developing minimum standards for space

and time out of cell, which both our domestic courts and, on the evidence to date, the ECHR, are unlikely to be able to develop.

2. Her Majesty's Chief Inspector of Prisons for Scotland

While the CPT functions in effect like an international **07–19** inspectorate, there has also been available since 1980, as described in Chapter 3, a domestic inspectorate of prisons. Conceived by the May Committee as a force which could bring a genuinely independent element into the regular running of penal establishments to ensure that they were operated in a way which accorded prisoners humane and proper treatment, the inspectorate has power to inspect all aspects of prisons and to report regularly to the Secretary of State. The chief inspector's reports on individual prisons, his annual reports and such special investigations as have been carried out by the inspectorate are all published, and, they provide an opportunity for informed discussion and assessment of what is being done in prisons.

It might be thought, however, that the Scottish **07–20** inspectorate has had little impact on developments in prisons. The English equivalent, especially under the leadership of Judge Stephen Tumin, has enjoyed a high public profile. Its routine reports on establishments receive wide coverage in the media; it has been asked to conduct several special investigations into incidents within prisons which have themselves attracted much media interest; their chief inspector has been asked to conduct inspections and investigations in foreign countries; he is also regularly invited to comment on prison affairs at public meetings and in broadcasts; and he jointly chaired the very public investigation into the riot at Strangeways prison, Manchester, which resulted in the Woolf Report. The inspectorate has used its "thematic reviews" to highlight issues like the need for the installation of integral sanitation in prisons, and improving grievance systems for prisoners. In contrast, Scottish reports have had scant media coverage and the inspectorate and its work have never attained the public profile of their southern equivalent. The Scottish inspectorate has conducted thorough inspections of individual prisons and produced good work on issues like social work in prisons, chaplaincy services and training for freedom programmes, but it does not seem to have developed the same breadth of approach to its mandate, and thus the potential to be at the forefront of improvements in prisons.

07–21   As other models for external inspection of prisons develop, it may be that the Scottish inspectorate will become a more pro-active body which will assist domestic developments, not simply to avoid adverse international comparisons but also to ensure that Scottish prisons can be held up as a model to other countries for both delivering and being seen to deliver justice and fairness to all involved.

Political Initiatives

07–22   Political awareness of prison conditions is unlikely to be a factor on its own in promoting improvements in the existing arrangements, though it should be borne in mind that both the new prison rules and the review of the grievance system featured among the commitments made in the Justice Charter. Imprisonment itself is from time to time a topic of political rhetoric, more often south of the border than in Scotland itself, but such rhetoric is most often confined to the alleged need to have severe sentences than to have changes in the conditions of imprisonment. Those in immediate charge of the running of prisons are relatively immune from political influence in the practices they adopt under the agreed policies, and this position is likely to become more secure with the move to agency status. There also appears to have been considerable harmony between the practitioners and their political masters in developing the new philosophy in Scotland, with much of the development work having been done by professional prison administrators.

Improved Staffing Standards

07–23   The increasing professionalism of prison administrators and prison staff in general is likely to be one of the major pressures for further reforms in prisons. As staff develop a sense of vocation towards their work, so must they see the need to improve both the physical and the psychological environment in which prisoners are kept. The philosophy espoused in *Opportunity and Responsibility*, especially the notion of the "responsible prisoner", can only serve to confirm the normalisation of prison conditions as a primary objective of the staff. While no form of deprivation of liberty can be "normal", the commitment to reduce the extent to which prison conditions have come to differ from those on the outside world is welcome. Not only will its implementation help to reduce the damage which imprisonment might otherwise do to the chances of the prisoner functioning normally in society on release, but it will also help to ensure that working conditions for prison staff themselves become more "normal".

Privatisation and Market Testing

There is much concern among prison staff about the possible   07–24
impact of privatisation and "market testing" in prisons. England has two private prisons at the time of writing, and a commitment has been made to put the running of a further six out to tender. Provision to enable the Secretary of State for Scotland to enter similar contracts is contained in the Criminal Justice and Public Order Act 1994. As part of the agreement in implementing staffing restructuring in 1994, it has been announced that there will be a suspension of market testing for four years. But plans are being made for a new private prison, possibly for remand prisoners. Some view these developments with alarm, seeing the inevitable consequences as a decline in the quantity and quality of staffing, and in all the services available to prisoners, as a private enterprise strives to maximise profits.

There is, of course, a moral or political question arising   07–25
from the move to privatise a function which many see as inherently a role of the state and one from which no individual should make a profit. Leaving that aside, however, it should be made clear that there is no prospect of any reduction in standards of accommodation or other facilities for prisoners being involved in the process. Given both our obligations under international treaties and the fact that no case can be made for exempting private companies from the provisions of the existing Act and Rules, there is no room for any such reduction. On the contrary, it is likely that any private sector involvement will be regulated by a contract which would require to specify detailed obligations and would contain within itself an enforcement mechanism to ensure that, in addition to the individual access prisoners

may have to complain about conditions, the State would be involved in some kind of inspection or monitoring system to ensure that the private company fulfils its contractual obligations. Accordingly, prisoners could well end up with better protections under such a system.

07–26   There are other benefits which could accrue from some form of privatisation. In the present economic climate, it is unlikely that substantial new prison building will be financed by government on its own. Much of the existing stock of buildings in Scotland is antiquated, and cannot easily be adapted to meet contemporary standards of, for example, sanitary facilities. Accordingly, if there is to be speedy progress on these fronts, new capital would be a great asset. Equally, many of the existing practices within penal establishments are the result of customs developed, by both staff and prisoners over many years, in the context of a monolithic state run system. One of the greatest difficulties facing the SPS is in managing the "culture change" demanded by the adoption of *Opportunity and Responsibility*. A new organisation being set up would not face the same burdens of history. And, finally, if a private enterprise did offer higher standards of facilities for prisoners, at the same time as meeting the expectations of society in relation to the functions of imprisonment, it would be difficult for the remaining public sector to avoid the example set by the alternative suppliers. It could be, of course, that privatisation would lead to the re-emergence of the patchy, and generally horrible, conditions prevailing under the local system of organisation of prisons at the start of the nineteenth century; but, in view of the legal controls now in place, such a development could not go unchecked.

The Place of the Law

07–27   The law has been both an active agent in producing change in prisons and a passive reflection of changes which have come about for other reasons. Although the state of the law is undoubtedly much better, in terms of protecting the rights of prisoners, at this time than it has been throughout the history of imprisonment in Scotland, there is no doubt that the law on its own cannot produce an acceptable prison system.

07–28   Ultimately good prisons are created only when there is a good relationship, based on mutual respect, between prison staff and prisoners. The best of physical conditions could not compensate for the absence of this. And good relationships are not something that can be mandated by legislation. It is true that good relationships cannot develop when all power resides in one partner and none in the other, or where one party perceives the other as acting arbitrarily, but it is equally true that legal justice is only a necessary and not a sufficient ingredient of a good relationship. Matrimonial law has been more successful at ending than at restoring marriages; neighbours resolving their differences through the courts are not likely to become the best of friends thereafter. But prisoners have to live 24 hours a day, seven days a week and 52 weeks a year in their prison, in the company of staff who could easily pass the equivalent of a very long life sentence spending most of their waking hours in the prison. Most prisoners would rather be somewhere else, and some may make constant and ingenuous attempts to realise that ambition. Some prisoners will continue to exhibit the behaviour, resulting from choice, circumstance or inability to cope, which brought them to prison in the first place. For both prisoners and staff, divorce is not a real option and uneasy cohabitation would quickly become intolerable. Law cannot regulate every aspect of their daily life; legal remedies cannot provide the solution to all the problems that may arise. Alternatives must work to ensure the smooth running of such complicated communities.

Given that the prison system can exercise no control over **07–29** which community members are provided on the prisoners' side, it must be careful to ensure that only the right people are recruited to the ranks of the staff. Then it must provide resources, in terms of training, facilities, support and equipment, to enable staff to perform their task with confidence and respect for everyone's dignity. Much more than good law and effective law enforcement mechanisms is required to produce the correct balance. But the law and legal redress mechanisms have an important role to play in providing a guarantee that minimum standards are maintained. Scotland has now reached a firm base in this regard; in the dynamic world of the prison, the base must be up to the challenge of constant change to remain relevant to the institution it is required to serve. We should, therefore, look for regular changes in the law described in this text.

SCOTTISH PENAL ESTABLISHMENTS

While section 10 of the 1989 Act, as substituted by section 22 of the 1993 Act, allows the Secretary of State to commit any prisoner to any prison, the main uses to which each establishment is put as at 1 November 1994 are described below. In all cases "short-term prisoners" and "long term prisoners" are as defined in the 1993 Act, that is short-term prisoners are those serving up to four years and long-term prisoners those serving four years or above.

HM Prison Aberdeen

Aberdeen, also known as Craiginches, acts as the local prison for the Grampian area with the exception of prisoners from Elgin (who go to Inverness) and holds short-term prisoners convicted within that area and remand prisoners from the courts within the area. It also takes remand prisoners from the Orkney and Shetland Islands. In addition to this main function, it also houses a small training for freedom unit and a unit for female remand prisoners. Its average daily population in 1993–94 was 137.

HM Prison Barlinnie (including HM Special Unit Barlinnie)

Situated on the same site, the main prison and the Special Unit, which is technically a separate prison, cater for markedly different functions. The main prison is a local prison serving courts in Glasgow, Lanarkshire, Stirlingshire, Ayrshire and some courts in Dunbartonshire. It receives both remand and convicted short-term prisoners from these areas. Some short-term prisoners are transferred to Low Moss. The main prison had a daily average population of 1,008 in 1993–94. The Special Unit accommodates a small number of selected long-term prisoners who are felt to be in need of the particular regime available in the Unit. It has been announced that the Unit will be closed in 1995.

HM Young Offenders Institution Castle Huntly

Castle Huntly, situated in Longforgan some seven miles from Dundee, is an open young offenders establishment catering for male prisoners between the ages of 16 and 21 who are in security category D. It had an average daily population of 93 in 1993–94.

HM Prison and Young Offenders Institution Cornton Vale

As the main prison for females in Scotland, Cornton Vale accommodates all females remanded or sentenced by the courts in Scotland except for a few remand prisoners who can be held in Inverness, Aberdeen or Dumfries prisons. The average daily population in 1993–94 was 171. Some efforts are made to keep young offenders, adults and remand prisoners separate within the establishment but, because of the small and varying numbers in each category, this is not always possible.

HM Prison and Young Offenders Institution Dumfries

The young offenders institution at Dumfries, also known as Jessiefield, provides high security accommodation for generally long-term, convicted young offenders. The prison provides a remand facility for the courts in Dumfries and Galloway for prisoners of every category, including a small number of females. The average population in 1993–94 was 133.

HM Prison Dungavel

Situated near Strathaven in Lanarkshire, Dungavel became an open adult prison in April 1994. Accordingly, all prisoners in Dungavel are now security category D and are generally long-term prisoners. The average daily population in 1993–94, when the prison also operated as a semi-open prison, was 113.

HM Prison Edinburgh

Commonly known as Saughton, HM Prison Edinburgh has four separate functions. First, it operates as a remand establishment for male prisoners committed by the courts of Edinburgh, Lothians and Borders, Kirkcaldy and Dunfermline. Secondly, it holds convicted short-term prisoners from the same courts. Thirdly, it operates as a national facility at the top end of the long-term prisoner system and, finally, it accommodates a training for freedom hostel. The average population in 1993–94 was 670.

HM Prison Friarton

Situated on the outskirts of Perth, Friarton is a low security prison accommodating a small number of category C adult male prisoners serving sentences of up to two years. The average daily population in 1993–94 was 65.

HM Prison and Young Offenders Institution Glenochil

Situated near Tullibody in Clackmannanshire, the Glenochil complex contains two separate institutions. The young offenders institution holds convicted young offenders serving up to two years and had an average daily population of 153 in 1993–94. The adult prison holds long-term convicted male prisoners allocated from other receiving establishments, usually towards the beginning of their sentence. The average daily population in 1993–94 was 379.

HM Prison Greenock

Greenock, also known as Gateside, has three main functions: first, as a remand establishment for adult males committed by courts located west of Glasgow; second, as the establishment holding prisoners detained under the Immigration Acts; and third, as an enhanced regime facility for long-term prisoners who have co-operated well in their original establishments. The average population in 1993–94 was 242.

HM Prison Inverness

Inverness Prison, also known as Porterfield, provides remand facilities for all the courts of the Highlands and Islands for both male and female prisoners. It also provides facilities for the detention of short-term male prisoners. Its average daily population in 1993–94 was 108. The segregation unit at Inverness, which has not been used for some time, is being transformed into a small unit for local vulnerable prisoners in 1995.

HM Remand Institution Longriggend

Longriggend Remand Institution situated near Airdrie operates mainly as a remand establishment for all males under the age of 21 remanded in custody by courts within Strathclyde and Central Regions. In addition, it holds a small group of convicted short-term adult prisoners serving less than two years who come from Barlinnie and carry out mainly domestic duties within the establishment. The average total daily population in 1993–94 was 183.

HM Prison Low Moss

Low Moss, situated near Bishopbriggs, provides accommodation for short-term convicted males of categories C and D most of whom are transferred to Low Moss from Barlinnie, though some come from Greenock and Edinburgh Prisons. The average daily population in 1993–94 was 359.

HM Prison Noranside

Noranside is an adult male open establishment, located near Forfar, which takes prisoners from all Scottish prisons. All the prisoners must be security category D before coming to Noranside, where they may be accommodated in the main prison or in the training for freedom unit. The average daily population in 1993–94 was 128.

HM Prison Penninghame

Penninghame is also an open establishment for convicted adult male prisoners from throughout Scotland. Situated near Newton Stewart, it had an average daily population in 1993–94 of 64.

HM Prison Perth

Like Edinburgh Prison, Perth has a variety of functions. It holds remand prisoners from Tayside Region and North Fife, convicted short-term prisoners from the same areas and long-term prisoners from throughout Scotland. It also has a training for freedom hostel and a small unit for disruptive prisoners who wish to reintegrate themselves into mainstream establishments. In 1993–94 it had an average daily population of 443.

HM Prison Peterhead

Peterhead accommodates two different categories of prisoner, a large group of prisoners who require to be segregated from mainstream prisoners for their own safety and a small group of prisoners identified as being disruptive or dangerous in mainstream establishments. It also has emergency accommodation available for up to 60 prisoners as a national resource. The majority of the protection prisoners are sex offenders and special programmes are run within the prison for this group of offenders. The average population in 1993–94 was 212.

HM Young Offenders Institution Polmont

Polmont provides accommodation for males in the age range 16 to 21. All offenders in that category sentenced to detention commence their sentence at Polmont. Generally those serving sentences of between one and four years remain at Polmont, subject to security considerations. There is also a training for freedom unit within the establishment. The average daily population in 1993–94 was 390.

HM Prison Shotts

The newest prison in Scotland, Shotts provides for long-term adult male prisoners, serving four years and over, who require to be kept in conditions of maximum security. Within the establishment, but technically a separate prison in its own right, is the Shotts Alternative Unit, which provides accommodation for a small number of long-term prisoners who have experienced difficulties in their normal prison of allocation. The total average daily population of Shotts in 1993–94 was 480.

INDEX